PAST, PRESENT & **FUTURES**

CHICAGO MERCANTILE EXCHANGE

The "Our Founder" bronze rooster statue signifies the humble origins of the Chicago Butter and Egg Board and, later, the Chicago Mercantile Exchange.

PAST, PRESENT & **FUTURES**

CHICAGO MERCANTILE EXCHANGE

JEFFREY L. RODENGEN

Edited by Ann Gossy
Design and layout by Ryan Milewicz

Dedicated to Magnus Lajtman, to whom I will always be indebted for introducing me to Cindy, who would soon become my friend, my confidant, and my loving wife.

WRITE STUFF

Write Stuff Enterprises, Inc.
1001 South Andrews Avenue
Fort Lauderdale, FL 33316
1-800-900-Book (1-800-900-2665)
(954) 462-6657
www.writestuffbooks.com

The publisher has made every effort to identify and locate the source of the photographs included in this edition of *Past, Present & Futures: Chicago Mercantile Exchange*. Grateful acknowledgment is made to those who have kindly granted permission for the use of their materials in this edition. If there are instances where proper credit was not given, the publisher will gladly make any necessary corrections in subsequent printings.

Publisher's Cataloging-In-Publication Data
(Prepared by The Donohue Group, Inc.)

Rodengen, Jeffrey L.
  Past, present & futures : Chicago Mercantile Exchange / Jeffrey L. Rodengen ; edited by Ann Gossy ; design and layout by Ryan Milewicz ; [foreword by Richard M. Daley].

  p. : ill., charts ; cm.

  Includes bibliographical references and index.
  ISBN-13: 978-1-932022-22-3
  ISBN-10: 1-932022-22-8

1. Chicago Mercantile Exchange--History. 2. Commodity exchanges--United States--History. I. Gossy, Ann. II. Milewicz, Ryan. III. Daley, Richard M. (Richard Michael), 1942- IV. Title. V. Title: Past, present and futures

HG6049 .R63 2008
332.644   2008923226

Completely produced in the
United States of America
10 9 8 7 6 5 4 3 2 1

Also by Jeffrey L. Rodengen

The Legend of Chris-Craft

IRON FIST:
The Lives of Carl Kiekhaefer

Evinrude-Johnson and
The Legend of OMC

Serving the Silent Service:
The Legend of Electric Boat

The Legend of Dr Pepper/Seven-Up

The Legend of Honeywell

The Legend of Briggs & Stratton

The Legend of Ingersoll-Rand

The Legend of Stanley:
150 Years of The Stanley Works

The MicroAge Way

The Legend of Halliburton

The Legend of York International

The Legend of Nucor Corporation

The Legend of Goodyear:
The First 100 Years

The Legend of AMP

The Legend of Cessna

The Legend of VF Corporation

The Spirit of AMD

The Legend of Rowan

New Horizons:
The Story of Ashland Inc.

The History of American Standard

The Legend of Mercury Marine

The Legend of Federal-Mogul

Against the Odds:
Inter-Tel—The First 30 Years

The Legend of Pfizer

State of the Heart: The Practical Guide to
Your Heart and Heart Surgery
with Larry W. Stephenson, M.D.

The Legend of Worthington Industries

The Legend of IBP

The Legend of Trinity Industries, Inc.

The Legend of
Cornelius Vanderbilt Whitney

The Legend of Amdahl

The Legend of Litton Industries

The Legend of Gulfstream

The Legend of Bertram
with David A. Patten

The Legend of Ritchie Bros. Auctioneers

The Legend of ALLTEL
with David A. Patten

The Yes, you can on Invacare Corporation
with Anthony L. Wall

The Ship in the Balloon:
The Story of Boston Scientific and the
Development of Less-Invasive Medicine

The Legend of Day & Zimmermann

The Legend of Noble Drilling

Fifty Years of Innovation: Kulicke & Soffa

Biomet—From Warsaw to the World
with Richard F. Hubbard

NRA: An American Legend

The Heritage and Values of RPM, Inc.

The Marmon Group: The First Fifty Years

The Legend of Grainger

The Legend of The Titan Corporation
with Richard F. Hubbard

The Legend of Discount Tire Co.
with Richard F. Hubbard

The Legend of Polaris
with Richard F. Hubbard

The Legend of La-Z-Boy
with Richard F. Hubbard

The Legend of McCarthy
with Richard F. Hubbard

Intervoice: Twenty Years of Innovation
with Richard F. Hubbard

Jefferson-Pilot Financial:
A Century of Excellence
with Richard F. Hubbard

The Legend of HCA

The Legend of Werner Enterprises
with Richard F. Hubbard

The History of J. F. Shea Co.
with Richard F. Hubbard

True to Our Vision
with Richard F. Hubbard

The Legend of Albert Trostel & Sons
with Richard F. Hubbard

The Legend of Sovereign Bancorp
with Richard F. Hubbard

Innovation is the Best Medicine:
The extraordinary story of Datascope
with Richard F. Hubbard

The Legend of Guardian Industries

The Legend of
Universal Forest Products

Changing the World: Polytechnic
University—The First 150 Years

Nothing is Impossible: The Legend
of Joe Hardy and 84 Lumber

In it for the Long Haul:
The Story of CRST

The Story of Parsons Corporation

Cerner: From Vision to Value

New Horizons:
The Story of Federated Investors

Office Depot: Taking Care of Business—
The First 20 Years

The Legend of General Parts:
Proudly Serving a World in Motion

Bard: Power of the Past,
Force of the Future

Innovation & Integrity:
The Story of Hub Group

Amica: A Century of Service
1907–2007

A Passion for Service:
The Story of ARAMARK

The Legend of Con-way:
A History of Service, Reliability,
Innovation, and Growth

TABLE OF CONTENTS

Following the close of the merger, CME Group Executive Chairman Terry Duffy and CEO Craig Donohue ring the bell for the first time as CME Group on July 13, 2007.

FOREWORD

BY

RICHARD M. DALEY
MAYOR, CITY OF CHICAGO

THE MERGER OF THE Chicago Mercantile Exchange (CME) and the Chicago Board of Trade (CBOT) is a landmark event for the City of Chicago. For more than 100 years, Chicago has earned a reputation as a global leader in commodities and derivatives trading, ranging from agricultural products to modern investment instruments designed to offset risk. The emerging CME Group Inc. has now secured Chicago's role as the undisputed global leader in risk management.

When the CME and the CBOT agreed to a common financial clearinghouse for exchange transactions in 2003, it soon became evident that by combining this strategic resource, the cost, speed of clearing, and confirmation of transactions would benefit both organizations. The new relationship also signaled a willingness to work together in an area that would ultimately reduce costs to the investors and financial institutions affiliated with both groups. When it came time to renew their joint clearinghouse relationship in 2006, an even wider conversation ensued, leading to the $11.2 billion acquisition of the CBOT by CME. The new entity, CME Group Inc. boasted more than $4 trillion in combined notional value of trades per day.

CME Group Inc. is at the forefront of the rapid growth of electronic trading, facilitating transactions that can be executed from any corner of the globe or securely from a personal computer. Its products are now available on a single electronic platform, CME Globex®, which will extend the reach of the new organization throughout the financial world. By combining, CME and CBOT have created an international financial power.

CME Group Inc. will fuel a growing economy for the City, more career opportunities for our residents, increased tax revenues to support our commitment to an expanded infrastructure, greater educational opportunities, and an improved quality of life for all. Congratulations to CME Group Inc. on your historic accomplishment.

May 19, 2008 was the first day of trading on the newly created CME Group trading floor. This new facility combines four major trading floors into one location and marked the last major milestone in the merger of the CBOT and CME to form CME Group. *(Photo by © David R. Barnes.)*

ACKNOWLEDGMENTS

MANY DEDICATED PEOPLE ASSISTED IN the research, preparation, and publication of *Past, Present & Futures: Chicago Mercantile Exchange*.

Research Assistant Danny Smith conducted the principal archival research for the book, while Senior Editor Ann Gossy managed the editorial content. Graphic Designer Ryan Milewicz brought the story to life.

Several key individuals associated with Chicago Mercantile Exchange (CME) provided their assistance in development of the book from its outline to its finished product, including: Terry Duffy, Craig Donohue, Leo Melamed, and Jack Sandner. Colleen Lazar served as the tireless and efficient corporate liaison. A special thank you goes to Mayor Richard M. Daley for contributing the book's foreword.

All of the people interviewed—CME employees, retirees, family, and friends—were generous with their time and insights. Those who shared their memories and thoughts include: Robert Abboud, Robert Aliber, Bill Brodsky, Charles Carey, John Davidson, Tad Davis, Craig Donohue, Terry Duffy, Ali Fatemi, Milton Friedman, Mitch Fulsher, Martin Gepsman, Phupinder Gill, Robert Glauber, Dan Glickman, David Gomach, Yra Harris, Henry Jarecki, Phil Johnson, Rick Kilcollin, Jim Krause, Barry Lind, Patrick Lynch, Randy McKay, John McPartland, Leo Melamed, Bill Miller, Michael Moscow, Steve Newcom, Carol Norton, Jim Oliff, Jamie Parisi, John Peschier, Todd Petzel, David Prosperi, Rick Redding, John Roberts, Thomas Russo, Jerry Salzman, Jack Sandner, Terry Savage, Myron Scholes, Verne Sedlacek, Charles Seeger, Bill Shepard, Beverly Splane, Hans Stoll, and Clayton Yeutter.

Finally, special thanks are extended to the staff at Write Stuff Enterprises, Inc.,: Stanimira Stefanova, executive editor; Elizabeth Fernandez and Heather Lewin, senior editors; Sandy Cruz, vice president/creative director; Elijah Meyer, graphic designer; Roy Adelman, on-press supervisor; Lisa Andruscavage, proofreader; Mary Aaron, transcriptionist; Elliot Linzer, indexer; Amy Major, executive assistant to Jeffrey L. Rodengen; Marianne Roberts, executive vice president, publisher, and chief financial officer; Steven Stahl, director of marketing; and Sherry Pawlirzyn-Hasso, bookkeeper.

1848—Chicago develops as agricultural marketplace; Chicago Board of Trade opens

1874—Produce dealers establish Chicago Produce Exchange (CPE), forerunner to CME

1912—CBEB moves into space at 136 Lake Street as exchange members assume full financial responsibility for transactions

1919—CBEB becomes the Chicago Mercantile Exchange (CME), a name anticipating futures trading of non-agricultural commodities, and establishes a clearinghouse in addition to revised bylaws

1865—Introduction of standardized futures contracts

1898—CPE disbands and morphs into Chicago Butter and Egg Board (CBEB)

SECTION I

BIRTH OF THE CHICAGO MERCANTILE EXCHANGE

(1848–1965)

1928—CME moves into new headquarters at 110 North Franklin Street

1958—Congressional ban on onion trading nearly halts the CME

1964—CME releases its revolutionary live cattle futures contract

1953—Everette B. Harris first named president of CME, replacing Oscar Olson

1961—CME introduces the frozen pork bellies futures contract, the first futures contract on frozen, stored meat

In 1898, the newly formed Chicago Butter and Egg Board found quarters at the Marine Building on LaSalle Street. The Board would call the Marine Building home until 1912, when it moved around the corner to 136 Lake Street.

CHAPTER ONE

ORIGINS OF THE FUTURES MARKET

1800s – 1911

The exchanges, obviously 19ᵗʰ century creatures, began somewhat as clubs, and that's how every exchange began. Like-minded men got together and traded things in coffeehouses, on curbs, or later exchanges.

—Charles Seeger

IT WAS PERHAPS ONLY NATURAL that Chicago would emerge as a major financial center, neither happenstance nor luck playing as dominant a role as location. With its close proximity to Lake Michigan and to the Mississippi River, its central location for railways, and its access to some of the nation's most productive agricultural sites, Chicago emerged as a market center for farmers in the mid-19ᵗʰ century. Corn, grains, and meats poured into the city from each direction.

Transportation, distribution, and trading of agricultural produce all found a profitable home in Chicago, from the first load of grain to leave the city limits in 1839, until the opening of the Union Stock Yards in 1865.[1] Add the city's increasing agricultural legacy to its growing attraction as a destination for various immigrant groups, each seeking to discover the potential the nation promised, and the stage was set for Chicago's rise to prominence as a key marketplace. There were folks eager to sell and products arriving in bulk to be sold. Indeed, the forces of supply and demand converged in Chicago.

South Water Street was most often the destination for buyers and sellers, a collection of street-savvy folk seeking profits. Known simply as The Street, South Water Street represented Chicago's earliest marketplace—fruit and vegetable dealers on the eastern end of the street, and meat, poultry, and dairy merchants blanketing the western end. It was where many of Chicago's famed early peddlers got their start, serving as a training ground for merchants to discover the ins and outs of business and trading. Long before exchanges became vast marketplaces for managing risk, there was only The Street, a firm handshake, and a man's word governing much of the day's transactions.

In 1848, the Board of Trade of the City of Chicago (later changed to Chicago Board of Trade—CBOT) was founded by 82 businessmen to represent the city's grain dealers, following the lead of similar institutions in Buffalo and Detroit. The CBOT became a common meeting place for merchants and businessmen to discuss all forms of business, including the formation of a commercial institution that would later become a major futures exchange. These discussions stemmed from the growing trade in Chicago and the recognition that an establishment was needed to apply fairness and equity to the marketplace.

The "Our Founder" bronze rooster statue signifies the humble origins of the Chicago Butter and Egg Board and, later, the Chicago Mercantile Exchange. Today, the bronze statue sits outside CME's executive offices and remains a symbolic feature for today's trader. It heralds traders back to simpler times, which gave way to the fast-paced movement of the 21ˢᵗ century.

Opposite: At the Chicago Board of Trade, one of the nation's founding commodities exchanges, grain dealers moved about the marketplace selling and buying. The success of the CBOT urged dealers in other goods, particularly Chicago's butter and egg men, to pursue their own exchanges.
(Photo by The Geo R. Lawrence Co.)

With the institution of the CBOT, investors seized the opportunity to build stockpiles of grain for year-round consumption, a decision that helped smooth out the grain supply problems—an abundance in the summer and fall, and short supply in the spring—and helped bring a certain measure of price stability to the commodity.[2]

All the while, Chicago continued its emergence as an agricultural hub, becoming a favored place to live as the nation's second-most populated city behind New York. Increasingly, merchants and distributors brought their goods to Chicago. In 1851, Chicago turned into the nation's primary corn market; in 1854, the nation's center for wheat; in 1860, the nation's largest lumber market; and during the Civil War, Chicago became the nation's largest meatpacking market.[3] Chicago had indeed arrived on the national economic map as a major player, and it had many of the resources—transportation, established marketplaces, consumers, and workers—to remain in the game.

Trading Receives a Makeover

Yet the ever-sprouting marketplace demanded continual evolution for merchants to keep pace. Most merchants relied on cash market contracts (called spot markets), in which buyers and sellers contracted for immediate delivery and payment of a certain commodity. But the practice soon became impractical. Trade expanded and many farmers entered the market at the same time, particularly during the period right after the fall harvest. Because the excess products overwhelmed transportation and storage facilities, the forces of supply and demand caused prices to drop dramatically. Meanwhile, the following spring would see severe commodity shortages and, again, guided by the basic forces of supply and demand, prices would spike dramatically.[4] The need for exchanges

FORWARD VERSUS FUTURES

AS DEFINED IN *AN INTRODUCTION TO Futures and Options* (Chicago: Chicago Mercantile Exchange Education Department, 2004):

Forward contract: A private agreement to buy or sell a commodity at a specific price on a specific date.[1]

Futures contract: A legally binding, standardized agreement to buy or sell a standardized commodity, specifying quantity and quality at a set price on a future date. Some futures contracts, such as the Live Cattle and British pound contracts, call for physical delivery of the commodity. Other futures contracts, such as the S&P 500 and Eurodollar contracts, are cash settled and do not have a physical delivery provision. If these contracts are not liquidated by the last trading day, the position is closed out by comparing its price against a special final settlement price and debiting or crediting the position accordingly.[2]

to handle the issues of storage, supply and demand, and fair trading practices surfaced as a way to further benefit those on each side of a deal.

During the latter stages of the 1800s, the idea of central clearinghouses gained credibility among merchants, financiers, manufacturers, and developers in an attempt to simplify the process so often clouded by legalese and jargon. The effort to utilize clearinghouses to standardize quality and define trade practices proved effective in creating a more efficient flow of commodities and trades.[5]

In 1865, the idea of standardized futures contracts materialized, a bright move away from a rather antiquated system. Increasingly, delivery dates and locations were determined—as were unit sizes and quality of deliverable goods—as forward trading continued its expansion in Chicago. These standard practices morphed into today's futures contracts.[6]

The Roots of the Chicago Mercantile Exchange

With the model provided by the nearby CBOT and the demand for basic commodities growing with the population, Chicago's butter and egg dealers sought to create their own exchange. On May 20, 1874, the Chicago Produce Exchange was founded, a modest precursor to today's Chicago Mercantile Exchange.

Just three years before, in 1871, the Great Fire destroyed Chicago's landscape and paralyzed the city, throwing its future into turmoil and uncertainty. Chicago rebounded, however, and in less than a decade was back on track expanding its social, political, and economic sights. The Chicago Produce Exchange was but one sign that the city was recovering amid its reconstruction. With renewed determination, Chicago moved toward becoming the nation's first great contemporary city, as well as home to the United States' futures markets.

The Chicago Produce Exchange opened at a hall on the northeast corner of Clark and Lake streets, and the membership soon reached 300. The Chicago Produce Exchange did little more than record trading statistics, a rather simplistic and elementary start; and due to inactivity, by 1878, its doors closed. However, after a brief hiatus, the Chicago Produce Exchange returned in 1882. The unpredictable market for butter and eggs held promise for many Chicago dealers because profits existed for the taking. With its emergence as an aggressive forwarding market, dealers organized to maintain their position in the market.[7]

THE HISTORY OF COMMODITIES MARKETS

IN THEIR EARLIEST KNOWN FORM, COMmodity markets emerged in ancient Sumeria where small baked clay tokens in the shape of sheep or goats were used in trade.[1] At the time, these trades were unreliable, and frequently feverish tempers arose from unmet expectations. Often, the goods never arrived, and disappointed recipients received any number of excuses. Other recipients complained of sick goats or naked sheep.[2]

Despite those frustrations, people continued to seek opportunities to standardize and trade contracts in various commodities, all in an attempt to achieve a more efficient and predictable process.[3] So, the archaic ways of ancient Sumeria's commodities market discouraged no one; the future of the commodities market remained intact.

While remnants of commodities markets can be traced to ancient Greek and Phoenician times as well, the first centralized futures market did not open until 1650 in Osaka, Japan, once the nation's major commercial center and a prime destination for many of the world's merchants in the 16th and 17th centuries. Japanese ruler Toyotomi Hideyoshi, encouraged merchants to move to Osaka—the nation's major port and marketplace—during the 1500s to further bolster the city's commercial livelihood.[4] There, agricultural commodities changed hands, and efforts to codify the practice took place as buyers and sellers continued attempts to balance and secure trade. Trust, however, guided much of the market action, while communication and credit in the marketplace remained primitive.[5]

The world's modern futures market, however, originated in the United States, particularly in Chicago with the 1848 establishment

The resurrected Chicago Produce Exchange established its headquarters at Clark and South Water streets, near the center of the marketplace bustle on The Street.

In the post–Civil War era, Chicago continued its growth, both as a burgeoning city with added land and inhabitants, as well as an economic marketplace for agricultural goods. During this period, Chicago boasted technological advances in the agricultural industry, including the invention of the refrigerated boxcar and progress in urban planning, such as the expansion of Chicago's harbor. The agricultural boom in surrounding states only furthered Chicago's boom.[8] As the nation's agricultural center, Chicago showed no sign of releasing its grip on the title. The city relished its agricultural position, fielding gallant new entrants into the industry.

It was in this promising environment that Max Weinberg went into business for himself. In 1879, a 12-year-old Weinberg arrived alone from Germany with the sole mission to bring his family to America. By 1885, after working as a busboy and in a meatpacking plant, Weinberg had saved enough money to secure arrival of his family from Germany and to start his own business venture. A young man with a clear entrepreneurial spirit, Weinberg first sold homemade sausages door-to-door and later joined with his brothers to create Weinberg Brothers & Company. The business, specializing in meat, poultry, and eggs, became America's oldest commodity firm owned by a single family. Weinberg, meanwhile, began to focus his attention in the direction of butter and egg futures.[9]

Another founding father of what would later become Chicago Mercantile Exchange was William S. Moore, a second-generation butter and egg wholesaler who learned how to grade and buy butter and eggs while working for his father after school

---

of the CBOT, and later the 1919 formation of the Chicago Mercantile Exchange, a by-product of the earlier Chicago Produce Exchange (1874) and Chicago Butter and Egg Board (1898). Throughout the 19th century, the founding American exchanges emerged as innovators for improvements in transportation, warehousing, and financing, all of which paved the way for expanded trade across the state and national borders.[6]

The major commodity was grain, and increasingly, urban centers located along the Great Lakes sought a more standardized market. The Buffalo Board of Trade opened in 1844, followed by the Detroit Board of Trade in 1847 and the CBOT one year later. By the middle of the 19th century, these associations and similar ones in other Great Lakes cities, such as Milwaukee and Cleveland, established a system of grading commodities and creating standards and inspections, all of which helped the trading process become more efficient and effective.[7] Further, the exchanges helped to stabilize often-volatile price fluctuations, resulting from supply surpluses and shortages throughout the year.[8]

In time, the exchanges gained credibility, as they brought a degree of consistency to trading practices. Still, detractors existed and the exchanges, both in Chicago and elsewhere, often were the target of criticism. Many individuals, from farmers to lawyers, thought that futures traders manipulated prices. Congress was frequently the battleground for such debates. In 1890, the Butterworth Anti-Option Bill was introduced in Congress, although it never reached a vote. Two years later, however, the Hatch and Washburn Anti-Option bills passed through both the House and Senate before failing on technicalities. The passage of either bill would have effectively signaled the end of futures trading in the United States.[9]

Despite the attacks, commodities trading evolved into a true barometer of supply and demand. Although the legitimacy of futures trading would frequently come under fire over the years, American exchanges held their ground, and for good reason. While today's futures world bears little resemblance to its rudimentary origins, the overwhelming truth remains steadfast: Futures markets help manage risk.

Above: One of the founding families of the original Chicago Butter and Egg Board, the Fox family, embodied characteristics of many members of the day—self-made types with an entrepreneurial spirit.

Opposite: The original Chicago Butter and Egg Board charter, as approved by then Illinois Secretary of State James A. Rose, in 1898. For nearly 20 years, until the formation of the Chicago Mercantile Exchange, the board would serve its butter and egg dealers well, while enduring various economic swings, including World War I.

and in the summers as a youth.[10] Among the earliest Chicago Produce Exchange members, Moore and Weinberg possessed personal characteristics representative of most members in the exchange— self-made, persevering, hard-working, and forward-thinking, with much personal stake in the exchange and its growth.

The First of Many Daring Moves

From its rebirth in the mid-1880s until the mid-1890s, the Chicago Produce Exchange moved along a steady track until frustrated butter and egg dealers began to question the exchange's wholesale pricing strategies determined solely by the exchange secretary. Each day, the secretary would informally poll selected merchants to achieve a consensus price. The secretary alone could decide whom to query and how to set the price, and the process did not sit well with many butter and egg dealers.[11]

Seeking a more democratic pricing system, Chicago's butter and egg dealers acknowledged the need to reorganize. In November 1895, they established the Produce Exchange Butter and Egg Board as a group within the Chicago Produce Exchange. Its single purpose was little more than to establish fair price quotations for its commodities.[12] The group chose leadership positions and held meetings once a week. With the egg market growing in both size and complexity, however, the trading of time contracts in eggs began to emerge as a real possibility.[13] Yet, for some, the time did not arrive soon enough, and the dissatisfaction sparked decisive action.

In February 1898, butter and egg dealers walked out of the Chicago Produce Exchange frustrated that butter dealers' attempts to win over legislation to support its industry were pounced upon by the exchange's margarine dealers. Meanwhile, with demand for refrigerated eggs on the rise, futures contracts in eggs seemed a logical path. As such, the Chicago Produce Exchange no longer met the needs of many of its members. In 1898, a group of renegade butter and egg dealers left the Chicago Produce Exchange and formed the Chicago Butter and Egg Board, soon after taking new space in the Marine Building at Lake and LaSalle streets. They offered the following objective upon their inception:

The purposes for which this corporation is formed are to establish for the benefit of its members daily market quotations on butter, eggs, and other products and to furnish general information to its members regarding the market for such commodities, and to facilitate the speedy adjustment of business disputes among its members, and to secure to its members the benefits of cooperation in the furtherance of their legitimate pursuits.[14]

Claiming 48 members, the Chicago Butter and Egg Board boasted such heavy-hitting, Chicago-based members as Swift & Company, Armour & Company, and Union Cold Storage Company. The new Chicago Butter and Egg Board elected four officers and expanded its Board with nine trustees, who served up to a two-year term.[15] Settled into its new Lake Street quarters, in May, at a moving expense of $150 and monthly rent of $27, the Chicago Butter and Egg Board immediately began to move its vision to action.

Its first line of business was to abandon official price quotations. The move, accepted by mem-

THE SHERMAN ANTITRUST ACT

PASSED IN 1890, THE SHERMAN ANTI-trust Act outlawed any contract, combination, or conspiracy in restraint of trade, while also prohibiting any person or business from monopolizing or attempting to monopolize any market. The antitrust law arrived as business tycoons, most notably John D. Rockefeller, brought many competitors under control in a trust, thereby eliminating most of the competition and strangling the free enterprise system in a given industry. Later, the trusts would lower production and raise prices, ignoring public outcry against such action.[1]

Monopolies were common in late–19th and early–20th century America. The major industries sought to squash the smaller merchants that blanketed much of the nation's landscape. In Chicago, the egg men banded together in an effort to ward off monopolistic expansion and those individuals attempting to unfairly control the market.[2] Despite its modest status, the egg was not immune to such monopolistic threats.

Ironically, however, the Chicago Butter and Egg Board was found guilty of controlling distribution of market information in 1915, under the Sherman Act. The law now was equally critical of the humble Lake Street establishment.[3] Though rearing its regulatory head into the Chicago Butter and Egg Board's quarters, the federal government nevertheless remained suspicious in regard to the futures markets' legitimacy and necessary place in the nation's economy. The public, too, joined in the misunderstanding.

This early battle served as a prelude of things to come. The exchanges, including Chicago Mercantile Exchange (CME), frequently found themselves the object of criticism and ire from Washington, D.C., to midwestern farms. Harnessing its resilient spirit, CME would secure its place and purpose in the national economy, lend credibility to the industry, and allow its continued status as a symbol of the "free markets for free men" ideal.

On February 16, 1910, Chicago Butter and Egg Board members gathered for a formal banquet at the LaSalle Hotel.
(Photo by Lawrence)

bers, signaled the Board's desire not to set the price of the commodity, but rather to "indicate the pulse of the market as a guidance for its members."[16] And so, the Chicago Butter and Egg Board moved forward, even if futures in egg contracts were slow to develop.

In little more than half a century, Chicago had emerged as the nation's marketplace for agricultural goods and other commodities, such as lumber. Chicago's marketplace gained sophistication, and its exchanges—the grain-dealing CBOT and the Chicago Butter and Egg Board—sought to keep step. But, with the ushering in of a new century, the form and purpose of commodities markets were making a transformation; no longer was the commodity of central

importance. Instead, the exchanges converted themselves into places in which the financial risk of price changes in either direction became the paramount concern over the actual commodity being traded.[17]

Additionally, there was a clear focus on giving a voice to all members, large and small. In 1905, the *Chicago Daily Tribune* acknowledged that without the trading pits, "the smaller men in the business would be hopelessly crowded out of the race by the big ones who would control the situation against them as if the market ceased to be an open one."[18] Nevertheless, a loud group of critics saw the exchanges as little more than gambling dens, a sign that the bucket shops (counterfeit "exchanges" that blossomed throughout Chicago) had indeed struck a blow to the legitimacy of both the CBOT and the Chicago Butter and Egg Board.

And while both exchanges would survive the first round of public relations battles, the Chicago Butter and Egg Board would lay the foundation for a century of innovation and progress to come.

Everette B. Harris (left) shares a laugh with Oscar Olson. A 35-year veteran of CME, Olson recruited Harris to join CME in 1953.

CHAPTER TWO

CME LEARNS TO WALK

1912–1955

Instead of constantly having to prove the value of a free marketplace, we can now devote our efforts to increasing the effectiveness of our exchanges by increasing their trade.

—CME President Everette B. Harris

IN 1912, THE CHICAGO BUTTER and Egg Board moved into new quarters at 136 Lake Street, in the heart of Chicago's expanding business district. All around, the city continued to take shape, and Chicago's butter and egg men soon set out to inform the growing city that somewhere amid the boom was a group called the Chicago Butter and Egg Board. This initiative alone would be work enough.

In October 1914, the Board placed an advertisement in the *Chicago Daily Tribune* suggesting that eggs and ham provided a real man's breakfast. Near other advertisements for linoleums and cigars, the Board's announcement employed the words of a government scientist, urging the public that cold-storage eggs, a new and improved method, were safe and of high quality, even if stored for up to eight months. The advertisement concluded with the image of a lean, debonair man dining on eggs over easy at the breakfast table.[1] A month later, the Board ran a similar advertisement in the *Chicago Examiner*. Chicago egg dealers handled more than 4.5 billion cases of eggs in 1914.[2]

Time contracts in eggs, however, were slow to develop. In the early 1900s, the vast majority of dealers avoided egg futures contracts. During volatile times in the egg market, contracts bounced around from dealer to dealer, subsequently lending credence to the purists' idea that time contracts would disrupt the character of the market.[3] Despite a minority that believed in the value of time contracts, the Board nevertheless moved to outlaw these contracts for a period of two months in the spring of 1915.[4]

Eventually, however, the minority's voice would be heard and the time for futures contracts would arrive in the present. By June 1916, time contracts were back in full swing at the Chicago Butter and Egg Board.[5] In 1917, the United States found itself fully involved in World War I. President Woodrow Wilson, citing broad executive wartime powers, began setting standard prices for many commodities and, along with others in the nation's hierarchy, proclaimed, "Food will win the war."

The butter and egg men on Lake Street felt the impact as prices of both commodities began to rise, along with trading in futures contracts, an activity still struggling to shed its negative label as a gambling operation. In a short time, trading in futures contracts was banned by the federal government, an edict that would remain until 1919.

CME introduced the onion futures contract in 1942. The *Chicago Daily Tribune* did not list CME's onion and egg prices until 1953.

The governmental ban on these contracts was lifted. The Chicago Butter and Egg Board took a proactive approach to help shed negative public perceptions, requiring all dealers to meet governmental regulations or face stiff consequences.

For many of Chicago's butter and egg men, however, the free enterprise system had yet to take shape. In 1919, a group of 10 influential butter and egg dealers presented a letter to the Board requesting changes to the rigid trading regulations. For example, one rule forbade traders from buying and selling on the call in the same session, while another limited sales on the call to spot transactions.[6]

Origins of Chicago Mercantile Exchange

In the spring of 1919, an informal meeting of dealers resulted in a thorough discussion of time contracts, the most heated issue of the day.[7] The open discussion, attended by the prominent likes of Oscar Olson, C. J. Eldridge, Charles McNeil, J. C. Borden, and Joseph Milnarik, led to one important point. The true value of time contracts had yet to be determined—even among the dealers themselves.[8]

In 1921, at its home on Lake Street, CME hosted 28 phones, as well as quote boards detailing the day's activities.

Seeking guidance on the subject, the dealers turned to William S. Moore, the day's foremost expert on the butter and egg business. Moore created a committee to gather information on the subject, seeking the counsel of both the Chicago Board of Trade (CBOT) and the New York Cotton Exchange. The findings made their way to the central committee, a group drafting the constitution for the new exchange. Moore convinced the Chicago Butter and Egg Board to add all of the findings on organized futures contracts to its rulebook.[9] A brilliant move by the confident Moore, it prevented a split among butter and egg dealers, thus allowing the shared goals of each merchant group to exist in a unified front.

The Chicago Butter and Egg Board ceased existence on Sunday, October 5, 1919, and gave way the following Monday morning to Chicago Mercantile Exchange (CME). This simple move proved wise as the day would soon come for the exchange to trade commodities other than butter and eggs.[10]

A Quiet Start

While the death of the Chicago Butter and Egg Board and the birth of CME proved a monumental event for Chicago's butter and egg dealers, it attracted little notice from its city. The *Chicago Daily Tribune*, the city's premier newspaper, made no mention of the new exchange's formation. During October's first full week in 1919, the only mention of any butter and egg business concerned a revived investigation by a U.S. prosecutor who discovered large warehouses of stored butter, while excessive prices were still being charged. In the minds of Chicago's newspapermen, CME deserved little ink. Meanwhile, the CBOT secured three *Tribune* headlines during the week, including talk of a new $5 million building at the foot of LaSalle Street.

At its Lake Street home in 1925, CME's administrative office employed a small group of dedicated workers in a modest space.

Nearly 150 Chicago Butter and Egg Board memberships were transferred over to the new CME, an organization committed to making up for lost ground in the organized trading race.

The most significant change came in the creation of a central clearinghouse, a move overseen by Board President Charles McNeil.[11] The clearinghouse, an idea with roots in the medieval fairs of the Middle Ages, represented a means of offsetting both money accounts and contractual obligations.[12] The clearinghouse helped much of the dealers' work move along in a more efficient and effective manner, as it saved clerical work and removed the burden of direct settlement. More than anything, however, the establishment of a clearinghouse in 1919 for CME business signaled the exchange's entry as a legitimate and forward-moving commodities exchange.

On the CME trading floor, the membership split into seven distinct groups, characterized by geographic location: the North Side, Fulton Street, Haymarket, New South Water Market, the Stock Yards on the South Side, the downtown Loop, and

the out-of-towners.[13] Rivalries sprung up, and fierce competitiveness dominated the trading pits. Some challenges among members proved so contentious that the existence of CME was threatened.

The seven distinct groups further complicated the continuing battle for organized trading versus the word-honored deals that once dominated South Water Street. The voices of visionaries who favored the benefits of organized trading and time contracts became louder. The traditionalists, those wishing the return to the handshake deals of South Water Street, were equally as adamant. Finally, in 1922, with discontent from both parties only growing, Moore and other exchange officials threatened to leave CME and form a new exchange. The mere warning started a dialogue and a compromise among the membership.

Traders from the 1920s gathered to conduct their business on the CME trading floor at 136 Lake Street. The blackboard system served as the sole system until 1945, at which time the CME Board instituted the auction-style market in addition to the blackboards.

Another New Home

With the city's widening of LaSalle Street, CME's headquarters at 136 Lake Street, just off the corner of LaSalle Street, would be forced to move elsewhere. CME's business manager, S. Edward Davis, sought the input of members. Strangely perhaps, one potential option involved moving CME into the CBOT's new $1.75 million quarters on LaSalle Street.[14] After much thought, CME leaders politely declined the offer, as much for the hefty rent the CBOT would charge as for the distinct culture of each exchange. Still, with the need for a new home growing—a home they could call their own—CME members rallied around plans for a new building at the corner of Franklin and Washington streets, a plot of land CME had purchased in 1922 for a little more than $500,000.[15] In a unanimous vote, nearly 300 exchange members approved the plan. Work on a new CME building would soon begin.

On April 26, 1928, CME opened the doors of its new home in grand fashion. The new CME included an expansive 75-by-125-foot trading floor with a 30-foot ceiling. Most noteworthy was the existence of free space without the interference of pillars. For the next 44 years, CME would call 110 North Franklin Street home.

The Great Depression Hits

In 1929, the price of a CME membership sold for a record $4,500,[16] and the nation's economic expansion continued. The prosperity seemed sure to maintain its smooth flow as the nation's economic fortunes hit a new peak in August. The tide of prosperity, however, began to slow, and within a few months, the United States found itself engaged in its most severe business collapse ever. Unemployment, the stock market, the gross national product, and factory output all moved in negative directions. A financial storm was about to knock the nation down, sending economic tremors from the kitchens of farm homes to the trading floors of the nation's commodities exchanges. CME would be forced to take measures to sustain its life. In the matter of one decade, CME would shift from a promising exchange gaining momentum in the futures industry to one seeking a rebirth from the Depression's wrath.

To add to the turmoil, CME endured a key management void when business manager Davis, a 40-year veteran of the butter and egg industry, retired. With government intervention lurking in the shadows, much as it had a decade earlier with the nation's involvement in World War I, CME turned east to the nation's capital for a replacement for the business manager post. Arguably

---

How It Looks From the Door

FLORENCE SHERMAN, OSCAR OLSON'S secretary, penned the following poem. As a female, Sherman could only watch the trading floor action from a door, since women were not allowed on the floor. The poem appeared in a 1926 issue of *Exchange News*, CME's monthly internal newsletter.[1]

One by one, they trickle in,
Some just quiet, some with din,
Some with lightly tripping toe,
Some with faces filled with woe.

And now approaches eleven o'clock,
The markets cease to roll and rock,
Hundreds of cars are bought and sold,
The record of which the world is told.

The bell has rung, the close at last,
The sound of conflict is ebbing fast,
The settlement price is posted too,
It cannot suit each one of you.

Now one by one they trickle out,
Some are sure, some are in doubt,
Some will gain, and some will pay.
Ah, well, tomorrow's another day.

CME's most crucial and influential administrative slot, this position required an objective outsider without membership ties. In 1930, CME found Department of Agriculture Economist Lloyd Tenny, a visionary with realistic sensibilities, who understood that the exchange's proper function should be to manage price risk.

At CME, with large quantities of butter and eggs accumulating, hedging became a tool for dealers

Above: To celebrate the opening of its new home at 110 North Franklin Street, CME invited humorist Will Rogers to speak at the dedication ceremony on April 25, 1928. With his characteristic charm on full display, Rogers entertained the crowd with such lines as, "So, get you some eggs and hold 'em. Somebody will eat 'em. If you can't pay your cold storage bill, hard-boil 'em and sell 'em for picnics."

Opposite: The Chicago Mercantile Exchange called 110 North Franklin Street home from 1928 until 1972. In 2003, the structure at the corner of Franklin and Washington streets was demolished.

looking to manage price risks. Shrewd dealers like Ludwig D. Schreiber, a legend of the era, found value in securing guaranteed futures prices. The influx of hedgers in the market lent to a decrease in speculators; subsequently, the necessary liquidity that had allowed the commodities business to run in an efficient manner had all but evaporated. Veteran egg dealer Alex Kittner reported that eggs sold for 10 to 12 cents a dozen, and dealers were eager to make ends meet where they could.[17] Later, in the 1930s, future CME Chairman Bill Katz recalled eggs dropping to as little as eight cents a dozen, and memberships were being auctioned off on the trading floor

for $100 after having reached a pre-Depression–era peak of $4,500.[18] Nothing in American history had ever touched off such panic and poverty as the Great Depression, and CME, like so many others across the nation's landscape, struggled desperately to stay afloat. CME leadership carried out bold moves, including cutting employees' salaries and liquidating the exchange's bond portfolio.[19]

Just as it had three decades prior, the U.S. military—some 12 million strong—required a range of commodities, including butter and eggs.[20] Though the pent-up surpluses of the Depression era vanished, CME President George B. Shawhan remained determined to see that CME members felt positive about their business, despite economic uncertainties. Led by Shawhan, the exchange introduced two new futures contracts in 1942— Idaho russet potatoes in April and onions in September. Also in 1942, CME expanded its Board from 12 to 15 members and, to increase objectivity in the boardroom, added directors from outside the butter and egg business.[21]

Enter Oscar and Optimism

In 1943, CME began searching for a replacement for Tenny and turned to the charismatic butter and egg man, Oscar Olson, as its new president.

At its new home on Franklin Street, CME traders eagerly engaged in the action on opening day, April 26, 1928. The expansive trading floor, which provided conveniently clear views of the blackboards, represented an upgrade from the cramped quarters of Lake Street.

Membership seats at the time sold for less than $300, and Olson sought ways to improve the health of the exchange. He met with the CME Board to discuss the exchange's postwar direction. Along with a plan to add new contracts, Olson proposed creating a budget for public relations and advertising.[22]

In January 1946, CME learned that President Truman would lift price controls on commodities one by one, based on supply and demand.[23] By October, the Truman administration lifted all price controls. CME could now return to full-business mode.

Throughout the later years of the 1940s, CME set about recapturing the lost momentum of the Depression and wartime years. In 1946, Charles

S. Borden, head of S. S. Borden and Company, a charter member of CME, replaced Maurice Mandeville as head of the CME Board, a group filled with veteran butter and egg men. In 1949, the aggressive advertising campaign Olson had conceived of years earlier began as the *Wall Street Journal* and other trade publications touted CME's activity.

Also, in 1949, CME released its newest futures contracts in dressed poultry and frozen eggs. With the progressive thinking of Chairman Harry Redfearn, who assumed the reins in 1949 and urged the old-time Board to think of the future, CME approached the 1950s with optimism and promise, as nearly 200,000 contracts per year were traded.

Exit Oscar and Enter E. B.

With retirement on his mind, CME President Oscar Olson actively sought his successor and found him, just up the street at the CBOT. Everette Bagby Harris responded to the call of a mutual friend, and soon after met Oscar Olson for lunch. Olson, then 64, had been with CME for more than three decades. He immediately proposed that Harris accept the leadership opening at CME. A surprised Harris relayed that he would consider the offer, while suggesting an even more courageous plan, a merger of the two Chicago-based exchanges. Olson and Harris parted and elected to brainstorm the respective proposals. A week later, Olson and Harris met again and quickly discarded the idea of a merger.[24] Harris, however, expressed an increasing interest in joining CME.

Though the CBOT was at the forefront of commodities exchanges, CME was still considered a wild card. While the CBOT was straightlaced and conservative, filled with affluence and confident of its elite

status, CME recognized its underdog status and fought for the respect it deserved.

A native Illinoisan with academic and business credentials to his credit, Harris claimed charm and wit along with the ability to interact effectively with a variety of people. Though an "outsider" to CME people, he possessed his own set of skills to add to the advancement of the exchange. During the early 1950s, Harris accepted Olson's offer and, in 1953, became the first official president of CME. Previously, the title of president remained with the chairman of the Board, but with Harris' arrival, the two titles would be separate.[25] For the next 25 years, Harris would serve CME as its president.

Though CME's trading volume had grown to 250,000 contracts annually, and a busy day would bring 5,000 trades, a fierce undercut punch soon would hit CME. The Dairy Products Marketing Association supported the postwar price of butter at

Bright lights from above illuminated the dynamic CME trading floor and its players in 1933.

LEO MELAMED JOINS CME

IT WAS BY PURE ACCIDENT THAT LEO Melamed, the man who would help revolutionize the futures industry, encountered the bustling world of Chicago Mercantile Exchange.

In the fall of 1952, a young student at John Marshall Law School named Leo Melamdovich was searching for a job as a morning law clerk at one of Chicago's many downtown firms. A Holocaust survivor who had trekked from his native Poland to Siberia and Japan before settling in Chicago's Humboldt Park neighborhood, Melamdovich sought the fulfillment of all that America promised. A friend directed him to an ad in the *Chicago Tribune*, where Melamdovich saw that the firm Merrill, Lynch, Pierce, Fenner, and Bean requested a "runner" between the hours of 9:00 A.M. and 1:00 P.M. The hours fit perfectly into the young student's schedule for whom law classes did not begin until 2:15 P.M.

The following day, Melamdovich arrived at 141 West Jackson, the announced address, and entered the Chicago Board of Trade. Though puzzled as to why a law firm would have offices in the Board of Trade building, Melamdovich nevertheless went through the interview process and was hired. He was told to report to 110 North Franklin Street the next morning, and ask for Joe Sieger.

Still convinced that the job had legal duties, Melamdovich abandoned that hope when he arrived at the Franklin Street location and saw a building labeled "Chicago Mercantile Exchange." He had never heard of the business, and upon entering the doors and traveling to the second floor, witnessed the free enterprise system in its organized flurry, as traders shouted and waved their hands. Captivated by the drama and its players, Melamdovich was intrigued and knew at that moment he wanted to be a player himself. He met Sieger, then the iron-fisted CME chairman and head broker for Merrill Lynch, and soon discovered that Merrill Lynch was a brokerage firm selling stocks, bonds, and commodities. Receiving his duties from Sieger, he took to his job, which was a position that would pay him $25 a week.[1]

In the immediate years to follow, Melamdovich, who changed his name to the Americanized Melamed in 1955, would not only learn the ways of the futures trading industry, but would also study the movements of his boss, Sieger. Increasingly, Melamed was pulled into the CME culture. Like so many others at CME, he was a product of modest roots with strict working-class values. He held idealistic hopes and considered himself an "allsy," either all long or all short on the trading floor. Moderate gains were not his business on the trading floor or in life. The hustle of life in the pits merged well with the action-seeking Melamed. He recalled:

The Merc was merely a means of getting through law school, I kept thinking. But I knew better. I had fallen in love with the place.[2]

Upon beginning his final year of law school in 1954, Melamed, then a 15-month veteran of the exchange, sought a more active role in the trading business. In short, he wanted to become a full-fledged member. With the cost of membership seats at $3,000, Melamed turned to his father for a loan. He then accompanied his father to CME and instructed him on the marketplace. With faith in his son, Isaac Melamed lent his son the necessary funds, and Leo soon after purchased his membership seat.

After graduation from law school in the summer of 1955, Melamed continued his double life trading on the exchange floor in the morning and practicing law in the afternoons and evenings. It was a life he would continue for the next 10 years. Melamed explained:

I hated it. I was a good lawyer. I was great in front of juries. I can emote. I'm an actor. I hated the whole profession. I hated the people I dealt with. I hated what I was doing. I was already bitten by the bug anyway. In law, I made money, but I eventually gave it all up to go trade.[3]

Above: This photo of the CME trading floor in 1956 shows not only the expansive nature of the floor, but also the flurry of activity characteristic of the free enterprise system at work.

Right: Apple traders in action on the CME trading floor.

25 cents per pound, effectively ending the exchange's trading in that product.[26] Left only with eggs, onions, potatoes, and poultry to trade, Harris drummed up support for CME by convincing the *Chicago Daily Tribune*, then only running the CBOT's daily grain prices, to add CME's onion and egg prices to its pages.[27] In a move that trumped traditional thinking, Harris also touted the advantages of commodities futures to the securities industry, a group struggling with its own bearish market.[28] In essence, Harris set out to convince anyone who might listen of CME's legitimacy and promise, particularly as compared to that of the stock exchanges.

Harris championed CME and the futures industry's benefits. He spoke of growth and poten-tial. He made information clear and succinct, tailoring it to meet the needs of a variety of potential audiences. And, most of all, Harris framed his words with confidence. The commodities business, he suggested, was the best game in town. In 1955, CME traded a record 550,000 contracts, and the price for a membership rose to $7,000.[29] Harris, it seemed, was right—CME could deliver its own boom, and people were beginning to notice.

By 1965, pork bellies surfaced as a hot commodity, and trading in live cattle futures continued to grow. The trading floor was becoming a far more active place after years of struggling.

CHAPTER THREE

CME'S FUTURES WORLD

1956–1965

We didn't know it couldn't be done.

—Everette B. Harris

CHICAGO MERCANTILE EX- change (CME) President Everette B. Harris was a man devoted to his endeavor. Upon assuming CME's leading role in 1953, Harris established as one of his primary initiatives a desire to educate others. The time of merely guessing what commodities exchanges did, reasoned Harris, had expired. From Chicago to Detroit, New York, and Kansas City, Harris guided training courses; spoke to journalists, economics clubs, and university groups; and provided insight on exchange business, allowing Harris to cast CME's net yet further onto the public domain.[1] While not crediting his actions as the primary contributor to the exchange's emerging success, he did conclude that business was moving in the right direction.

Back at 110 North Franklin Street, CME continued shaping its identity and searching for the proper business model. For most of the 1950s, only two of the floor's three trading pits saw activity. With the disappearance of butter, the exchange placed its fortunes on onions, eggs, potatoes, and turkeys.

Still, CME wasn't necessarily all business. Despite some frenzied moments in the trading pits, in which competitive juices would run high, traders created a clublike atmosphere with card games and table tennis contests.

The Great Onion Debate

In 1957, Harris journeyed to Washington, D.C., to appear before the Congressional Joint Economic Committee.[2] In previous years, the National Onion Growers Association and individual farmers claimed that price speculation was having an adverse effect on the onion. Harris met with congressmen to explain the legitimacy of futures trading and to ward off talk of an impending ban on onion trading.

Despite Harris' best-laid plans, as well as Illinois Senator Paul Douglas' defense of futures trading, Congress sent its own message when it enacted the Onion Futures Act on August 28, 1958. For the first time in the nation's history, futures trading in a commodity was outlawed; the onion was no more.[3] None of Harris' goodwill mattered much to Congress, a group that often blamed futures exchanges for fluctuating prices and what was perceived as an inability to self-regulate. Harris would later confess that the punch

Part of CME President Everette B. Harris' master plan for the exchange was to increase visibility regarding its business, which meant participating in traveling road shows and displaying exhibits, such as this one in Las Vegas.

Traders bought and sold in the onion pit in the late 1950s. After the government enacted the Onion Futures Act in 1958, the onion pit closed. It was the first time in the nation's history that the government banned futures trading in a commodity.

delivered by the Onion Futures Act "was almost fatal to the exchange."[4]

On the CME floor, traders wondered what would become of the exchange, once moving toward progress, but now hit with a ban on its second-most traded commodity. Only a few years before, butter trading had ceased, and now the onion, in an unprecedented government edict, would be erased from CME's blackboards. CME's future, it appeared, rested on the fragile egg—both storage and frozen— and members noted the precarious situation.

After Congress handed down the Onion Futures Act, CME leadership considered next steps to advance its purpose. Exchange leaders debated taking the legal route, a battle that held the potential to land in the United States Supreme Court. CME engaged Archibald Cox, a Harvard Law School professor and constitutional lawyer, as outside counsel. Cox questioned CME leaders on exchange history and regulatory issues.[5] Throughout the conversation, Harris reminded both Cox and the CME Board that futures trading served a necessary mechanism to forward the nation's economic machinery.

In the end, Cox advised CME to avoid fighting the onion ban in court. He argued that a negative Supreme Court decision would leave CME and other futures exchanges vulnerable to excessive government regulation. A negative decision from the nation's highest court could threaten the vitality of commodities markets altogether.[6] In a vote, the Board concurred with Cox's judgment and decided that the potential benefits of a victory paled in comparison to the risks associated with losing.

Although Harris would later voice regrets at not pursuing the legal battle, he would nevertheless honor the Board's vote and resolve to help shape the exchange's future path. For Harris, that meant conducting more road shows, as he sought to repair CME's shaky public image and restore a sense of purpose and legitimacy to exchange business. Harris knew, too, that CME needed new life, and he urged membership to provide it.

Prior to Christmas 1958, Harris shared a letter with the membership calling upon everyone to do their part in repairing the damage and promoting the benefits of the futures industry. He concluded by asking members for suggestions for new commodities.[7]

Research Brings Results

Harris created a business conduct committee to address the issues involving additional advertising and educational campaigns and matters of self-policing. With membership seat prices falling alongside trader morale, CME members turned to a trusted colleague, John V. McCarthy, a charter member of the exchange with more than a half-century of exchange experience to his credit. McCarthy, and later Harris, noted that the onion controversy had so crippled the exchange that the future was all but forgotten. If CME desired to move ahead, new blood and new contracts would have to accompany it on its upward journey.[8]

In 1961, Bill Katz, a former CME chairman and veteran of the futures business, again assumed the chairman's post at a time when CME struggled to survive. Certain commodities had died, others were teetering on the brink of extinction, and others simply were never popular from the start. Despite the bleak outlook, CME refused to call it quits at little more than four decades old. Instead, an exchange's committee charged with researching new contracts would thoroughly investigate the viability of each contract before it

came to the trading floor. In the spring of 1961, the committee introduced its first proposed contract— pork bellies. Katz wondered aloud:

What the hell is a pork belly?[9]

Strange name notwithstanding, the exchange began trading contracts on pork bellies (slabs of bacon) in 1961.[10] In addition, the Board launched a publicity campaign to educate the public about pork bellies. On September 18, 1961, the pork bellies futures contract opened on the CME trading floor. The CME Board was convinced that the new contract would be the exchange's savior.

Pigs and Cows on the Floor

Initial results on the new pork belly contract were far from stellar—less than 1,000 contracts traded in the first 16 months.[11] CME leadership nevertheless maintained optimism. The forces of supply and demand, contended Harris, would exert their power in due time.

Meanwhile, the exchange continued researching new contracts. Harris proposed a futures market in Florida orange juice concentrate and followed that idea with a pecan contract. Both plans were dismissed. On April 1, 1962, CME's contract on iced broilers opened but, within a year, it joined butter in the commodities graveyard. In November 1963, CME opened trading in frozen shrimp. By the end of 1965, the shrimp contract had sunk.[12] All the while, pork bellies continued to flounder on the trading floor. Suddenly, pessimism even worked its way into Harris' generally hopeful mind; the president announced his impending resignation in late 1963. All signs pointed to a slow death for Chicago Mercantile Exchange.

Responding to the Board's pleading request for him to remain president, Harris reconsidered his retirement and soon afterward signed a five-year contract with CME.[13] Meanwhile, trading in pork bellies caught fire as the nation's demand for bacon merged with a declining pig population. By mid-1964, the exchange experienced a financial upturn as a result of its success with pork bellies.

CME then opened its latest contract on November 30, 1964. Before 9:00 A.M., Harris,

CME brought a live steer to the trading floor in honor of the opening of the live cattle futures contract.

along with fellow CME employee Susan Kein and Beef Cattle Committee Chairman Glen Andersen, walked onto the exchange trading floor accompanied by a Black Angus steer, a symbol of the nation's $10 billion livestock industry.[14]

At the time, trading in live cattle futures was a revolutionary concept. Despite mixed opinions from cattlemen and meat industry insiders about the potential for such a contract, Harris was convinced that trading in a live commodity would work. CME, he argued, could function as it always

had, by serving as a vehicle for others to manage price risk. A commodity was nothing more than a product someone wanted, Harris contended, and people wanted products that came from live cattle. It was enough to justify a futures contract.

CME staff turned to CME veteran Milt Stern to devise the delivery agreement for the live cattle contract, a progressive concept that required some imaginative thinking on Stern's part. Leo Melamed, who in 1969 would become CME chairman, commented:

Thank you, Milt Stern. Cattle was the first contract to be delivered in futures on the hoof. Everything else was stored items, you know. Grain was stored. Pork bellies were slabs of bacon. Everything was stored. Milt Stern assigned this delivery on the hoof for the first time at CME. If I were to suggest that we have a history of innovations, you've got to start with that point.[15]

By the end of 1965, CME had pulled itself out of its desperate position. No longer struggling for survival, the exchange had made positive strides by adding hogs and cattle to its futures listings. Frozen pork bellies accounted for more than 600,000 con-

tracts in 1965, and the exchange traded 900,000 contracts that year, nearly double CME's previous record year in 1960. The cost of a membership, a sign of an exchange's health, also reached a new high of $15,000, more than a $10,000 jump from the previous year.[16] Most notably, member apathy, at an all-time low following the onion ban and unstable futures outlook, was gone.

The Seeds of Change

Clearly, frozen pork bellies had all but saved CME, and life in the trading pits was improving. For some on Franklin Street, however, the business revival served only to show how much potential the exchange possessed. As John V. McCarthy had commented years before, the onion fiasco not only extin-

---

CME unveiled the frozen pork belly contract on September 18, 1961. Within six years, the contract became one of the nation's most actively traded commodities.

Opposite: On February 15, 1965, CME unveiled yet another new contract—this one in dressed beef. CME President Everette B. Harris (right) shook hands with Chairman Stephen Greenberg in celebration of the commodity's opening.

guished the life of a popular commodity, it also temporarily silenced CME's bold pursuit of the future. Now, amid the growing prosperity of CME business, there were members clamoring for a voice, a slice of CME's future fortunes.

Throughout much of its history, the CME Board constituted a who's who of ties to Chicago's original butter and egg men. For some exchange members, the time had arrived to inject not only new blood into the exchange's hierarchy, but also new policies and programs. The vast majority of the exchange's rulebook had remained intact, although the nature of trading had changed dramatically from butter and eggs to pork bellies and live cattle.

Above all else, however, new members wanted a voice within the old guard system. Although business at the exchange was on an upswing, many members not previously involved in CME's inner circle wanted to make certain their ideas were heard.

Not long before, as CME faced its bleak prospects, a group of young traders, some who bought their memberships on handshake loans and desperately needed CME to survive, shared their gripes. The youthful group of upstarts led by Leo Melamed came to be known as the Young Turks, and they intended to wrestle the destiny of CME from the old guard. Amid the tough times, the Young Turks sought to change the requirements for a special meeting. With reform on the mind, the group set out to obtain proxies for the special meeting, the first time such a task was attempted.[17]

The Board voted to lower the quorum to 100 members (from the previous 300) to call a special meeting.[18] The victory for the Young Turks represented a breakthrough, as they were able to amend CME's archaic ways democratically; furthermore, it served as the first victory in a lengthy and stressful internal battle for the exchange's future control.

As the 1960s rolled ahead, the calls for change, emerging voices, and new leadership grew, along with CME's future potential.

1966—CME introduces the
hog futures contract

1970—CME rewrites its rule book,
establishing a new era

1972—CME moves into new $6
million headquarters at 444 West
Jackson Boulevard

1975—CME merges with
the IMM

1968—Leo Melamed is elected
to the CME Board, setting the
stage for his near four-decade
run of CME leadership

1972—Following the collapse of the
Bretton Woods Agreement the previous
year, CME creates the International
Monetary Market (IMM) and begins
trading foreign currencies, effectively
altering the way in which the world
manages its risk

1974—Congress establishes
the Commodity Futures
Trading Commission (CFTC),
the first U.S. government
agency overseeing the
trading of futures

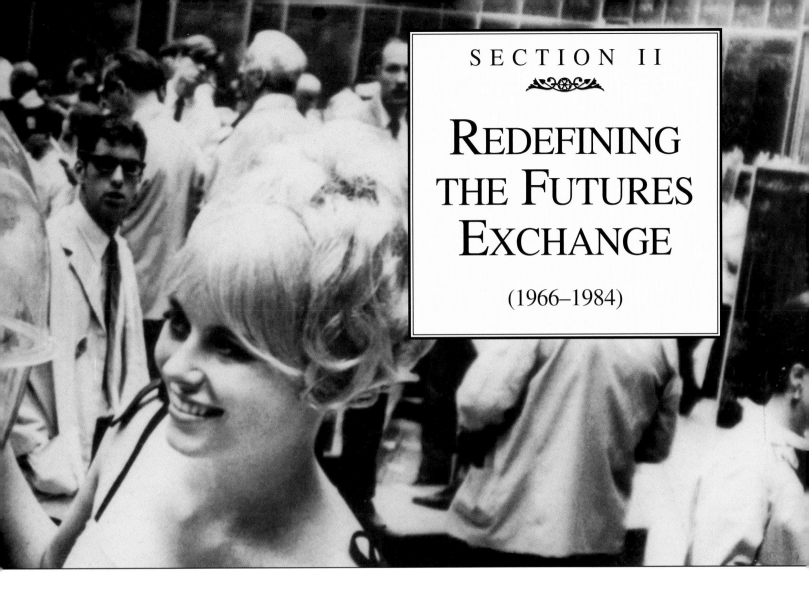

1976—CME introduces the first short-term interest rate futures contract based on 90-day Treasury bills

1980—CME opens London office, thereby becoming the first U.S. futures exchange to open a foreign office

1984—CME establishes the first successful international link between futures exchanges with Singapore Derivatives Exchange (formerly known as SIMEX)

1982—CME creates Index and Options Market (IOM) and launches first and most successful stock index futures contract, the S&P 500 futures

1978—CME opens an office in Washington, D.C.; Clayton K. Yeutter replaces Everette B. Harris as CME president

1981—Certificate of Deposit contract begins trading July 29; Eurodollar futures trading begins December 19, establishing the first futures contract to be cash settled

1983—Construction ends and trading begins in CME's new $350-million Wacker Drive home

CME members Gerald Hirsch (left) and Robert J. O'Brien hold a pair of hogs to commemorate the opening of the live hog futures contract at CME on February 28, 1966.

CHAPTER FOUR

A FINANCIAL REVOLUTION

1966 – 1972

The IMM [International Monetary Market] was not out to beat anybody and we were not trying to resurrect or reinvent something. This was pure invention—new market territory for an era in transition.

—Leo Melamed

AS THE LATTER YEARS OF THE 1960s pressed on, Chicago Mercantile Exchange (CME) continued to introduce new futures contracts. With the emergence of its live cattle futures contract, CME was convinced that trading a live product not only could be successful for the exchange business, but could be a viable tool for the industry as well. Increasingly, hedging emerged as an intelligent play, allowing the market for live products to maintain a consistent energy as hedgers matched speculators to forge a forward-moving liquid market.

On February 28, 1966, CME opened trading in live hogs. And, just as Everette B. Harris and CME had celebrated the opening of the live cattle contract with a steer on the trading floor, they would celebrate the opening of live hog futures with a chorus of hogs squealing.

In less than five years, CME had introduced three futures contracts—pork bellies, live cattle, and live hogs. All three proved successful.

Calls for Change Demand an Answer

Despite the positive turn in fortunes, many CME members still desired a business culture in which their voices could be heard. Challenges to CME's old guard began as early as 1961 when a group known as the Young Turks passed the quorum for special meeting requirements. Future years, however, would show that little had changed as the old guard continued its affairs without participation from younger members. Input from committees and special groups had little effect on exchange operations.

Finally, in 1967, and with unrest growing among the silent majority, the Young Turks resumed their efforts to effectively alter the Board's composition. But first, they would challenge the referendum bylaws. In addition to making the Board more responsible to its members, they wanted the membership to have a more active voice.[1] In essence, the Young Turks put on their boxing gloves and called the leadership into the ring.

In December 1967, an organized debate on the trading floor ensued between CME hierarchy and the Young Turks. Leo Melamed, a native of Poland who had escaped his homeland upon German invasion and began at the exchange in 1952 as a $25-a-week runner, found himself at the center of the action representing the Young Turks' appeal for Rule 206.

One of the most democratic bylaws ever discussed among exchange membership anywhere, Rule 206 effectively called for the Board to share the

In 1971, CME President Everette B. Harris celebrated the 10th anniversary of the frozen pork bellies contract with humor.

power of creating and eliminating rules with the exchange membership.[2] With spirited rhetoric, Melamed explained that the Board was legally bound to the referendum and championed its passage. Less than an hour later, Rule 206 was adopted by the membership. Melamed said:

> *We needed to create a culture in which the speed of change constantly rose and questions were allowed to be asked. This was a member-owned institution, not a private club. And it dealt with a public and business world outside of its doors. It had to be accountable. That meant that the Board had to be accountable to the members, to the exchange, to the users of the Merc.*[3]

For his efforts, Melamed emerged a rising star among the membership, was elected to the Board in January 1967, and was joined by new Chairman Robert J. O'Brien as an ally to the Young Turks' cause.[4] O'Brien's appointment was of critical importance as he blended the exchange's old guard (he was the son-in-law of veteran butter and egg man John V. McCarthy) with the new blood seeking to import orig-

A young Leo Melamed spoke at CME's 50th anniversary celebration, held at the Lincoln Park Zoo. Melamed emerged the point man in CME's shift from the old guard to new blood in the late 1960s. In 1969, Melamed gained the membership's top post when he was elected chairman.

inal ideas and a healthy dose of reform. O'Brien committed to creating a new image for CME, in addition to fashioning a future plan of action.

Leo in Charge

In February 1968, CME expanded its trading area by 25 percent and furnished the elongated space with new catwalks and ticker booths, nine double desks, and six 12-foot teletype enclosures. The exchange also instituted a new IBM data processing center and new trading boards.[5] The cosmetic changes, however, were not the only adjustments. Chairman O'Brien recognized the Young Turks' claim that the bylaws were both outdated and out of sync with the current market.

O'Brien served as the perfect balance between the fundamental mission of the exchange, its history, and the fresh ideas circling about. As CME recorded new highs in trading volume, O'Brien tightened the reins to create a more efficient and self-policing business. He increased fines for infractions, strengthened rules on accounts, and upped the financial requirements for clearing members.[6] Despite these strides, many assumed that CME soon would land in the hands of the Young Turks.

On October 5, 1969, as Chicago Mercantile Exchange neared its half-century mark, Leo Melamed, the impassioned young trader who made a name for himself in the exchange's political structure, entered the office as exchange chairman at the age of 36—its youngest chairman. He set forth three goals: to rewrite and update CME's bylaws, to change CME's image by cracking down on those traders who tried to manipulate the markets, and to diversify the exchange by creating new markets.[7] Melamed said:

As chairman, I not only wanted to keep the momentum going but I also concerned myself with the long-range view. You can short the market, but you can't be shortsighted running an exchange.[8]

Although CME ranked as the nation's second-largest commodity futures exchange, and membership seat prices rose to an all-time high of $32,000, it nevertheless, reasoned Melamed and various other members, needed some modernization along with decisive plans for the future.[9] The Board, with the addition of new leadership, had the challenge of determining CME's future path.

While the Young Turks' uprising initially caused bitter feelings among the older generation, those feelings eventually subsided as the established members saw the passion Melamed and others exhibited for the exchange's liveli-

In 1968, marking the fourth anniversary of trading in live cattle futures, CME Chairman Robert J. O'Brien (right) presents a cowboy hat to Joey Bishop (center) on his national television show. O'Brien and CME Vice President of Public Relations Ronald Frost (left) also presented Bishop with a champion steer that was later auctioned for charity.

hood. Without question, CME was an organization entangled in questions of stability, but it was determined to move forward.

"The Merc was to become not simply a place of work, but a place to love, too. I wanted the members to participate as well, to feel the Merc's new energy and zeal," said Melamed.

Rewriting the Rules

Rewriting CME's rule book was one of Melamed's top priorities. This was not a revolt against the past, but rather an intense recognition of the present and future of the exchange, an organization that needed more member involvement. As chairman, some worried Melamed would immediately overhaul the CME staff and direction, including the post of CME President Everette B. Harris. These concerns were unwarranted. Melamed set out to conduct research of his own and concluded that continuity served a central purpose to CME's future. He would, however, reorganize and redefine many of the exchange's departments and instill a need for a diligent and loyal attitude toward exchange business. As new committees emerged, a prerequisite for increased member involvement, CME aggressively forged ahead with a central concern—the archaic bylaws.[10]

As 1969 pressed on, CME celebrated its 50th birthday in grand fashion. The Board's plan for diversification helped push the exchange to new heights. Pork bellies bypassed corn as the nation's most traded commodity, while Idaho potatoes, a revised egg contract, a modernized live cattle contract, hogs, hams, turkeys, boneless beef, and lumber all contributed to the exchange's new face. For the first time in its history, CME surpassed the Chicago Board of Trade (CBOT) in volume, with more than $39 billion in contracts changing hands.[11]

By the turn of the decade, CME had emerged as a major player in the nation's futures industry, a sign evident by the flurry of activity on the trading floor. Despite its progress, CME still struggled to achieve respect from the industry's major players, including the neighboring CBOT and many of New York's financial heavyweights.

Lloyd F. Arnold (left), chairman of CME's cattle committee, and John T. Geldermann, chairman of the floor facilities committee, study the exchange's new electronic quotation board for live cattle. In late 1971, seven electronic boards were introduced displaying opening and closing ranges, the year's high and low prices to date, and recent transactions.

Perhaps most impressive, a seat at CME jumped to an astounding $90,000, far surpassing everyone's hopes that CME could celebrate its 50th year with a $50,000 membership.[12]

Furthermore, the $1 million expansion of trading space completed earlier in the year had already been deemed too small. Talk turned to a new headquarters to accommodate CME's rapid evolution.

Yet, all the good fortune refused to give way to the business at hand. CME leaders remained committed to the vision of building the nation's premier commodities exchange. While the United States battled inflation and a potential recession during the early Nixon years, CME considered its future, undertaking plans to create the world's most modern commodities exchange. Still, CME leaders would not be distracted from the organization's main purpose—business—and foremost to that end was the revised rule book.

After two years of committee work, the guidance of lawyer Jerold E. Salzman, much compromise, and extensive legal work, each CME member received a copy of the new rule book on June 1, 1970.[13] The old rule book, held together with tape and paper clips, contained contradictions and scribbled writing amid its unexplained revisions.[14] If nothing else, the old rule book was well-intentioned. So, too, however, was this refashioned model, one containing a system of checks and balances. One noteworthy change involved the integration of a Business Conduct Committee with power to police the exchange. Nearly every rule had been modified with great care: Some were merely reworded for clarity, others revised in concept.[15]

The "free markets for free men" mantra now boasted a well-written set of democratic guidelines to support the claim it so championed through the years. Within two years, Melamed realized a pair of his stated goals as he joined with others in rewriting the rule book and pushing self-regulatory initiatives.

"I knew where the Merc was at that point and, more important, I realized its enormous potential. And I knew something else, the days of winking at trading violations were over," said Melamed, offering further credence to leadership's plans that CME would be a place of business integrity.[16]

Yet for all of its expansion and progress, CME would still experience its best days ahead. The pork belly boys, a reminder of poet Carl Sandburg's description of Chicago as "hog butcher for the world," would soon shake the foundation of the commodities world. In effect, CME would spearhead a financial revolution, thus accomplishing Melamed's third stated objective—diversifying CME's markets.

Although the 1960s had been a time of immense growth and ever-expanding visibility, CME was still viewed as a minor-league player even in its own town, a city dominated by the prestige and influence often wielded by CBOT. CME led the nation with nearly $40 billion worth of contracts traded in 1969, but its success failed to gain the respect CME members felt it deserved.[17] Still viewing CME traders as a group of hog and cattle traders, outsiders dismissed them as inferior players among the commodity market's elite. Despite major steps to alter its shaky image, the

COHEN'S BOLD ADVERTISING

UPON ELECTION TO CME PRESIDENT, Everette B. Harris identified education and advertising among his primary aims. In 1969, with the winds of change sweeping through Franklin Street, Harris and CME, spearheaded by Publicity Committee Chair Gerald Hirsch, turned to Martin Cohen, who headed a one-man advertising agency and boasted broad knowledge of the futures market. Soon, CME's advertising budget, at the urging of Cohen, moved from $25,000 to $100,000 a year. Cohen drafted a series of advertising campaigns that earned high marks from some and criticism from others.[1]

Cohen developed some of his campaigns based upon remarks Leo Melamed made while testifying in defense of the futures market. At one point Melamed commented, "How come there is no Peking duck exchange?"

Cohen's first ad for CME focused on the emergence of the pork belly trade as he displayed the image of a portly pig with the words "Capitalist Pig" emblazoned below; a later advertisement depicted British philosopher Sir Francis Bacon with the caption "Sir Francis Pork Belly."[2] Though some CME members did not enthusiastically support Cohen's imaginative creations, a true break from the fairly rigid financial advertising at the time, the exchange realized the benefits of Cohen's aggressive advertising style. As a result, the Cohen–CME relationship continued for nearly two decades.

The bold advertising campaign produced results, too. Interest in the futures market soared to an all-time high, perhaps most evident by an ad in *Playboy* that yielded some 900 queries about the greatly unknown futures industry. The strong response from the *Playboy* ad, coupled with enthusiastic interest from other ads, furthered CME's targeted marketing approach. Though acknowledging the risks involved in the futures industry, CME and Cohen continued to pour out advertisements at an impressive pace. The message: CME was a place of active business and energy, and it had a compelling story to tell. Cohen's advertising campaign made sure people listened.

---

exchange still faced unsubstantiated charges that its floor hummed with speculators looking to make a quick buck. In time, CME would answer each of its critics with a resounding, offensive strike.

The Pieces Come Together

Above all, the shifting fortunes of CME in the late 1960s could be traced to its innovative take on old business. The momentum began with the frozen pork bellies contract—the nation's first futures contract on frozen, stored meat. By 1968, just seven years after its introduction, pork bellies were one of the most actively traded commodities in the nation. Soon after, the live commodities—cattle and hogs—furthered CME's product depth with successful trading. Only a decade before, CME had stood on the brink of extinction. By the turn of the decade, however, it emerged a major national player by creating and trading bold contracts

before anyone else arrived on the scene. Throwing the idea of failure aside, CME leaders from Leo Melamed to Everette B. Harris joined with the exchange membership to continue the forward march with a resilient and exuberant spirit.

Not content with present success and unwilling to fall in lockstep with the nation's other exchanges, Harris led efforts to land a skilled economist who could help the exchange's continued promotional efforts in the financial community and add insight to the creation of new contracts. In 1969, the search ended when they hired Mark J. Powers, PhD, a 31-year-old University of Wisconsin economist who not only boasted dairy farm roots, but also completed a doctoral dissertation on pork belly futures.[18]

Powers, the world's first economist employed directly by a futures exchange, was fascinated by the exchange business. His fascination increased when Harris instructed Powers to forget the agricultural staples so dominant on the exchange boards in favor of gold and foreign currencies. Harris' edict sprouted from the insistence of Melamed, the young chairman who held visions of merging the world of finance with the swirl of the pits. Melamed recalled:

> *Here I was, chairman of an exchange, desperately looking for diversification, and trying all these oddball and crazy contracts with dubious potential. Why not turn to finance? I couldn't let [the idea] go ... All my instincts told me that the world of finance could be better applied to futures markets than to the world of agriculture.*[19]

The 1971 Board of Governors and exchange officers, the group that pioneered the opening of the IMM and set a new course for CME (from left): Mark J. Powers, PhD, vice president, research and education; Ronald J. Frost, vice president, public relations; Carl E. Anderson; Robert J. O'Brien; Gerald Hirsch, first vice chairman; Laurence M. Rosenberg; Everette B. Harris, president; Leo Melamed, chairman; William C. Muno, secretary; Kenneth B. Mackay, executive vice president; John T. Geldermann; Michael Weinberg, Jr., second vice chairman; William M. Phelan, vice president, audits and investigations; Barry J. Lind; and Lloyd Arnold. Absent are Daniel Jesser, treasurer, and Marlow King.

In March 1971, Melamed introduced the notion of currency futures to CME's Board. Indeed, Powers concurrently contemplated the same idea. So Powers joined Melamed in supporting it. Among the Board members, however, controversy ensued on the feasibility of such a concept. Melamed said:

> *If Bretton Woods were to fall apart, then a currency futures market would work. And CME could provide this market with facilities, communications, public participation, and know-how. It could bring together buyer and seller.*[20]

The financial fates smiled upon the Franklin Street establishment. Bretton Woods, the World War II–era agreement that tied the world's major currencies to the U.S. dollar, began to crumble, thus making the idea of currency futures one with a good deal of potential. All the idea needed was some additional nudges to reach the market.

Nothing Gold Stays

During the winter and spring of 1971, the world's currency system stood in near disarray. In a tightly bound forward market, only large banks and foreign exchange dealers maintained the ability to dabble in foreign currencies. Private speculation, with its

MILTON FRIEDMAN REMEMBERED

RENOWNED ECONOMIST Professor Milton Friedman, PhD, served as a tremendous ally and force for Chicago Mercantile Exchange (CME) since the relationship began in 1970.

As economic advisor to President Richard Nixon, Friedman urged the U.S. leader to close the gold window upon entering office in 1969.[1] While Nixon initially vetoed the idea, he later honored the professor's advice in 1971, as the multinational Bretton Woods Agreement crumbled. Friedman's support to CME regarding FX futures served to spearhead the currency futures revolution, thereby redefining the commodities industry.

Often labeled "the mentor of the International Monetary Market (IMM)," Friedman experienced his own personal battle with the tightly knit foreign currency market in the fall of 1967. With the idea that Great Britain would soon devalue its currency, Friedman first called a Chicago bank seeking to sell short $300,000 in British pounds while guaranteeing $30,000 in cash as a security deposit. The Chicago bank declined the offer, and two major New York banks similarly followed suit. Speculation in foreign currencies, Friedman was told, earned disapproving glares, particularly from the Federal Reserve Bank and the Bank of England.

Just as he had predicted, Britain devalued the pound within three weeks of his initial inquiry. If allowed his transaction request, Friedman, an opponent of fixed exchange rates, would have doubled his money.[2] The

frustration Friedman encountered with the banks would compel collaboration with Leo Melamed and CME when discussions of the IMM arose in the spring of 1971.

Melamed, who once said that Friedman "was like a god" to him, leaned heavily upon Friedman's advice and reputation as the IMM emerged from theory to reality.[3] If not for Friedman's championing of the currency futures market, Melamed admitted, he would have been hard-pressed to go it alone.

In 1976, Friedman received the honor of ringing the bell for the opening day of trading Treasury bill futures.

Friedman, who taught at the University of Chicago from 1946 to 1976, earned the 1976 Nobel Memorial Prize honor for economic science. In 1977, he left the University of Chicago to join Stanford University's Hoover Institution as a senior research fellow. His work in monetary history and theory continues to receive tremendous credibility among the financial world and has earned him wide acclaim.

Friedman, considered by many to be the most influential economist of the 20th century, died on November 16, 2006, at the age of 94. CME and the University of Chicago hosted a memorial service to honor Professor Friedman on Monday January 29, 2007, declaring it "Milton Friedman Day." The event celebrated the economist's positive impact on American life and business and the spread of the benefits of free markets to nations around the globe.

potentially negative effects on exchange rates, was held at a distance. Meanwhile, the international currency speculators—an unknown group—shifted falling U.S. money into stronger foreign currencies such as the West German deutsche mark and Japanese yen.[21] Soon after, West Germany and Japan floated their respective currencies, a direct violation of the International Monetary Fund, the multinational organization charged with overseeing the Bretton Woods Agreement.[22]

On August 15, 1971, U.S. President Richard Nixon responded to the currency chaos with his own bold dictum: The United States was closing the gold window. For the first time in history, every nation claimed an irredeemable paper standard.[23] Nixon's decision served as the impetus to kick CME's plan for introducing foreign currency futures into high gear. Later, in December 1971, finance ministers from some of the world's leading industrial nations gathered to draft a new monetary agreement. The United States devalued the dollar while raising the price of gold. Other nations, meanwhile, adjusted their currencies to meet the U.S. dollar. Yet most intriguing to CME was the decision to permit a 2.25 percent fluctuation—in either direction—of exchange rates against the U.S. dollar. With that move, CME readied its plans to trade in foreign currencies. A wider price fluctuation window allowed for more action in the trading pits.

Meanwhile, in Chicago ...

Powers, still settling into his post on Franklin Street, continued to investigate the possibilities of trading in foreign currencies.

"I said to Mark Powers," recalled Melamed, "figure out what the specifications of these contracts ought to be, what size and denomination and all that. The next morning on my desk were all the specifications in the contract."[24]

Melamed and CME found a partner in the respected University of Chicago economist Milton Friedman, PhD, who had predicted the fall of Bretton Woods for more than two decades.[25] Although Dr. Friedman remained hopeful of the potential for trading in foreign currencies, he nevertheless admitted to not knowing for certain if the idea would work. For Melamed, the mere

encouragement of the renowned Dr. Friedman was enough to further pursue the idea.

Harris and Melamed traveled to New York to meet with a vacationing Dr. Friedman. CME's purpose was simple and direct. The exchange needed Dr. Friedman to stand in their corner. For $7,500, an investment regarded as the finest ever made in CME history, Dr. Friedman agreed to write a study on the subject.[26]

Just as the world's major finance ministers gathered in Washington, D.C., in December 1971, Dr. Friedman's 11-page study was released. Dr. Friedman and CME had successfully predicted the wider range of price fluctuations, and within two weeks, at Melamed's initiative, the International Monetary Market (IMM), an arm of CME, gained its business charter from Illinois. The IMM became the world's first market organized exclusively for the

In leaving his post as chairman of CME, Leo Melamed (right) handed the chairman's gavel to Michael J. Weinberg, Jr. A veteran of the CME political structure, Weinberg assumed the chairmanship in early 1972 after stints as secretary, treasurer, second vice chairman, and head of various committees.

On May 16, 1972, IMM Chairman Leo Melamed (center) stood with (from left) CME Chairman Michael J. Weinberg, Jr., Chicago City Controller David Stahl, International Monetary Fund Executive Director William B. Dale, and CME President Everette B. Harris to commemorate the opening of the IMM, a concept that would revolutionize the commodities world and change the way the world manages risk.

trading of financial futures. Dr. Friedman, meanwhile, would emerge a devout ally of CME business, as well as the trusted sage during future growth of the IMM and CME. Dr. Friedman commented:

The more important evidence was what the market did. The IMM had said there is a need for some way in which individuals can trade foreign exchange. That need was certainly demonstrated by the reaction of the establishment of the IMM.[27]

As the idea of currency futures trading sparked curiosity elsewhere, members of CME's Foreign Currency Committee continued their effort to integrate the new futures offering. Eventually, the committee established a firm set of guidelines. The IMM was to be a separate exchange operating within the CME building, restricted to dealing solely in monetary instruments. Furthermore, current CME members would receive an IMM membership for a small fee, and outsiders would pay a more substantial cost.[28] While trading in currencies was certainly a novel endeavor—the plan nevertheless spoke to CME's core—it provided a hedging mechanism for those seeking to protect themselves from risks. Trading in currencies allowed speculators an opportunity as well.[29]

Birth of the IMM

On December 18, 1971, CME held a press conference disclosing its plans, with Harris, Melamed, and Powers at the forefront. CME stood alone in the

foreign currency business. Outsiders claimed that CME was out of its league; in truth, various members, including some of CME's leaders and some on the Board, even wondered if the plan would work. Recognizing the need to lend credibility to its plan, Melamed recruited a new cadre of IMM Board members with influential names in the financial field—men with strong credentials and others from powerful banks—such as Robert Abboud from First National Bank of Chicago and Beryl Sprinkel from Harris Bank, as well as Henry Jarecki, PhD, chairman of the Mocatta Group, the world's largest gold and bullion dealing company. Abboud explained:

The rest of the world kind of pooh-poohed the idea. The bankers pooh-poohed the idea. I thought it was a great idea because the pressures were such that we needed some sort of mechanism where liquidity and spreading risk could basically establish the disciplines, which governments and central banks were unable to do.

The risk really became: Can this institution, which had been trading in pork bellies, eggs, and agricultural commodities, put together the plumbing and the financial aspects to be able to handle this as a contract?[30]

Similarly, IMM Board member Jarecki expressed concerns over the viability of trading in foreign currencies, particularly with the heavy hand of the banking community hovering over the IMM's moves. "I was skeptical whether the banking community would embrace it, or what they would do to interfere with it. It was clear that this was sort of their own fiefdom up to that time," said Jarecki.[31]

On January 17, 1972, CME members approved the creation of the IMM by a vote of 321 to 19. CME members were immediately allowed to purchase an IMM seat for $100, thus allowing the

IMM a built-in trading base. The public, however, would pay $10,000 for a chance to trade currency futures.[32] Melamed then assumed the reins as the IMM's first (and only) chairman.

"The idea was to create a separate exchange, an adjunct to Chicago Mercantile Exchange, using the same floor and board markers and administration and people, but called the International Monetary Market, the IMM, of CME. And the IMM had no limit," Melamed said.

But the IMM chairman recognized something else as well. He needed to encourage more traders to join, tapping into a younger generation eager to try their hand at the commodities market. The one-year $10,000 IMM membership was a step in that direction. Melamed said, "I was trying to attract [younger guys]. Come. ... Maybe you're an accountant. Maybe you're this. Maybe you're that. Ten grand. Get ten grand. Come on board. These were the guys who built the IMM."[33]

No turning back now, the IMM would open in less than four months. Powers penned the contract specifications, while Continental Bank's John McPartland handled the design for delivery.[34] Immediately, Melamed toured the United States and Europe on behalf of financial futures and the IMM, touting its new potential.

"We launched the revolution in 1972 against everybody's belief. And except for Milton Friedman, [we] might not have done it, but Milton Friedman loved it so, and embraced it so, and said it was a great idea," said Melamed.[35]

Others shared the vision that upstart CME would indeed create one of the world's most revolutionary financial concepts. Abboud said:

I had the confidence in both Everette Harris and Leo, and the people at the exchange—that if they said they could put in the plumbing and the actual mechanics of how to do the marketplace—that they would be able to do it. Sure, I knew there might be some mistakes in the beginning as you begin to fabricate the thing. But in the end, I knew they'd do it. So, in my mind, I was really playing to their expertise on the mechanical aspect of things, and on the other side, really sharing in their vision that basically the market would embrace this—that we could get out to the ultimate value assessors, which is really the broad financial public around the world.[36]

Ribbon Cutting

The story of the modern Chicago Mercantile Exchange—and for that matter the modern futures market—begins on May 16, 1972. On that day,

Traders readied for the opening of the IMM. The opening day of the IMM witnessed 333 currency contracts traded, beginning with Charles Mattey's purchase of two million British pounds from Henry Jarecki, PhD's, Mocatta Metals Corporation. By the end of 1972, more than 140,000 contracts changed hands on the IMM floor.

WOMEN AND CME

FROM ITS INCEPTION UNTIL 1966, CHIcago Mercantile Exchange was a man's world—and a man's world alone. Men blanketed the trading floor in suits, ties, and hats, sometimes with cigars dangling from their lips. Women were relegated to looking only through the door. Not a rule singular to CME, futures exchanges across the country similarly prohibited women from being on the trading floor.

Eventually, Sandra J. Stephens shattered the male-dominated world when she took to the trading floor as a clerk for R. J. O'Brien and Associates, Inc.[1] Some dispute does exist regarding this claim to fame, however, as Lois Berger Knight maintains she broke the gender barrier at CME a full seven years prior to Stephens when Knight worked as a phone clerk for John E. Coleman at CME.[2] The disagreement aside, the fact remains that CME became a socially progressive institution among the nation's futures exchanges by first allowing women on its premises.

It was not, however, until 1972, that a female entered the pits as a trader. Carol Norton, a petite woman whose career started at Leo Melamed's Dellsher clearing firm, stands as the exchange's first female trader when she, at the suggestion of her bridge-playing partner, Melamed, purchased an IMM seat for $10,000.

"I made $70 [on a trade during my first day] and I thought I was God's gift to the financial world," Norton said. "Everybody asks me, 'What was it like to be the first woman?' It was fun. I don't think anybody knew I was a woman. I was a trader, which was important."

For its part, CME, once again a forerunner, became the first futures exchange to open membership to women.

IMM Chairman Leo Melamed was joined by CME Chairman Michael J. Weinberg, Jr., Chicago City Controller David Stahl, International Monetary Fund Director William B. Dale, and CME President Everette B. Harris to commemorate the opening of the International Monetary Market, a daring new venture that had the world watching with considerable interest. British pounds, Canadian dollars, deutsche marks, Swiss and French francs, Japanese yen, Italian lira, and Mexican pesos were all traded on the blackboard.[37] At day's end, 333 contracts were traded.

On the very day of Melamed's ceremonious ribbon cutting, the *Wall Street Journal* quoted one New York bank foreign-exchange dealer as saying:

I'm amazed that a bunch of crapshooters in pork bellies have the temerity to think that they can beat some of the world's most sophisticated traders at their own game.[38]

Today, CME integrates that comment into their modern visitors center display, a nod to the underdog mentality that whirled about the exchange in the early days of the IMM. Indeed, not only did Melamed and his colleagues have the gall to bring foreign currencies into the pit, but they also outwitted and outplayed the competitors in the process.

In reflecting upon the IMM's formation a decade later, CME Chairman Jack Sandner would say, "The IMM is a story written by individuals inspired by a vision based on the ideals of free enterprise. Surrounded by a world of doubting Thomases, the story of the IMM began with this vision and a leap of faith that the vision would be realized."[39]

One key step in the IMM's success occurred when the exchange offered banks a class B membership of arbitrageurs. The idea was to maintain a liquid market between the IMM and the banks.[40] IMM leaders understood that if the market was successful, then class B arbitrage would become extinct, so the risk was minimal. More banks, reasoned Melamed and other leaders, would not only further the market but advance the IMM's credibility and potential as well.

On November 22, 1972, CME staff and traders posed one last time on the Franklin Street trading floor. CME called 110 North Franklin Street home from 1928 until 1972.

"I think clearly the introduction of financial futures changed the nature of the exchange as well as the whole industry," said Mitch Fulscher, an Arthur Andersen auditor who worked closely with CME and Melamed beginning in 1969. "It certainly brought in an entirely different audience and participant, namely the financial community became involved. It became very clear that the nature of the futures industry was changing as a result of [the IMM]."[41]

A Modest Start

By the end of 1972, the IMM traded a formidable 144,928 contracts.[42] Though not necessarily the phenomenal success leaders envisioned, this new market was up, moving, and gaining momentum along with credibility. Upon its inception, Melamed had reminded others that the IMM was a decade-long plan that required patience.

"What Leo and CME did was create a whole industry," said Thomas A. Russo, chairman and chief legal officer for Lehman Brothers. "Futures markets were not just there for commodities. Future markets were there for a purpose—price discovery and hedging. So it went from what was traded to the concept of trading itself. That was the huge leap and that was the genius in getting it done. People wrote about it, and all that, but CME did it. I think that's the remarkable thing."[43]

For young traders like Bill Shepard, who came to CME in January 1971 to work for his trading cousin Larry Shepard, the early IMM days were slow ones, but not ones filled with despair. Bill Shepard explained:

Unfortunately, it was very difficult to make anything trading the IMM products at the time due to lack of volume. They were brand new. [CME mem-

bers] who had faith in what was created sat on their hands, and some of them did more than sit on their hands. Some of them took young kids, young employees, badged them up with an IMM seat, and said walk around, stand in that pit, and basically make bids and offers instead of going out on a break.

So some of these guys would go into the pit and make bids and offers for an hour and make no trades, but at least if customer business came by, there might be a bid there, there might be an offer there, that the customer could be satisfied with.[44]

Also in the exchange's favor, a shift away from stocks and into the commodities business began to pervade the nation's financial psyche. In 1972, for the first time in the nation's history, the dollar value in commodities topped the dollar value in stocks traded by a substantial $53 billion.[45] Suddenly, entry into the IMM and CME was a hot ticket, a fact made evident when membership costs topped $100,000.

In the IMM Annual Report, Melamed shared his perspective with members: "If we succeed with currencies, the sky's the limit."[46]

According to Dr. Friedman: "The fact that an individual, a private individual, could go to market and put in an order for marks or francs or yen, or something else, and get a transaction right away, that was, by all odds, the most important thing, and that has been the foundation."[47]

Professor Milton Friedman, PhD, rang the opening bell for the Treasury bill futures contract on January 8, 1976. The T-bill contract, based on 90-day Treasury bills, was the first short-term interest rate futures contract listed on any futures exchange.

CHAPTER FIVE

INNOVATION NEVER SLEEPS

1973–1980

The IMM [International Monetary Market] was like money itself—it took on value because people had confidence in it.

—Leo Melamed

AS TRADERS LEFT 110 North Franklin Street on Wednesday, November 22, 1972, scurrying home in anticipation of the Thanksgiving holiday, they did so knowing that Chicago Mercantile Exchange's (CME's) long-time Franklin Street headquarters would remain with them, but only as a memory. Progress demanded a larger space, and the coming Monday's journey into the pits would lead them to the other side of Chicago's Madison Avenue, four blocks south and a block-and-a-half west of the historic Franklin Street structure.

"To move an entire exchange is no small undertaking," said Leo Melamed, who, as chairman, oversaw the moving process to the new Jackson Boulevard headquarters. "We knew of no such previous moves, and we knew how many things could go wrong."[1]

The concern evaporated when, on Monday morning, November 27, 1972, CME opened the doors to its new home along the west bank of the Chicago River, a $6-million architectural gem designed by Skidmore, Owings & Merrill LLP, that, with its steel and glass construction, resembled the first six floors of the city's famed John Hancock Building. CME furnished its new dwelling at 444 West Jackson Boulevard with all of the latest technology and up to a dozen trading pits with no interior walls or columns on the 25,000-square-

foot trading floor. A marvel to the eye, it also was a clear sign as to how far the sleepy exchange had traveled since its more modest butter and egg days.

"The traders were ecstatic over the new premises," said Melamed. "It was as if we had left the Dark Ages and entered the Promised Land. Everything was modern, bright, brand-spanking new, and in the right place."[2]

Trader Alex Kittner, who earlier reminisced about the opening of CME's Franklin Street home in 1927, told the *Chicago Tribune*, "I was sick when the old building closed last Wednesday. But today, well, what can I say but that I'm happy. We've experienced such fantastic growth."[3]

Yet growth arrived in many forms. At CME, where membership prices neared six figures, and the estimated value of contracts traded in 1972 would reach close to the $60-billion mark, eager traders embraced the progress and the possi-

---

In November 1972, CME moved into its new headquarters at 444 West Jackson Boulevard. The building garnered the slogan "The house that pork bellies built" in an ode to CME's popular product that all but resurrected exchange business in the 1960s. The modernized new home, designed by Skidmore, Owings & Merrill LLP, boasted a column-free, 25,000-square-foot trading floor with 21 futures and options contracts available for trading.

IMM Chairman Leo Melamed (right) rang a model of the Liberty Bell held by CME Chairman Michael J. Weinberg, Jr., officially opening trading at the new CME home on Jackson Boulevard, as CME President Everette B. Harris (left) looked on.

bilities.[4] The expansive Jackson Boulevard headquarters signaled the health of the exchange.

After the ceremonial ringing of a miniature Liberty Bell that arrived direct from Boston, *Chicago Tribune* journalist Edward Lee reported, "It was now business as usual, the same commodities, the same personalities, only a different trading floor."[5]

A Little Patience, a Little Luck

The physical move, however, would be but one overriding symbol of the significant changes that the exchange would eagerly grasp throughout the decade. The fledgling International Monetary Market (IMM), still months away from its first anniversary, brought new traders into the pits, many of them both starry-eyed and hungry for financial action.

Soon, however, the IMM began to hit its stride. Just like pork bellies a decade before, a persistent attitude splashed with some luck served to make the necessary combination. As the IMM neared its first birthday in 1973, economic turmoil rattled the world's financial legs, including the oil embargo and the Arab–Israeli War. Oil prices surged, as did inflation and the price of gold, while the Dow Jones Industrial Average and U.S. dollar endured sharp declines.[6] All the financial mayhem and activity elevated the IMM to a position of validity and necessity. The first full year of the IMM, 1973, witnessed nearly 420,000 contracts changing hands. Melamed commented:

It exceeded my wildest expectations. There was no doubt in my mind that the International Monetary Market was an idea whose time had come.[7]

Of course, luck played its part. Indeed, if I could have ordained the perfect backdrop for the creation of a new financial futures exchange designed to help manage the risk of currency and interest rate price movement, I could not have done better than what actually happened.[8]

The Golden Step

In his 1973 Annual Report to the members, Melamed wrote, "Our new market was specifically designed to encompass as many viable trading vehicles in the world of finance as practicable. We must be willing and ready to explore all possibilities."[9]

On December 29, 1972, CME President Everette B. Harris (left) shared champagne with (from left) Thomas O. Rockefeller, W. E. Hutton general partner; Michael J. Weinberg, Jr., CME chairman; Arthur Raitano, W. E. Hutton vice president; and James Barbi, W. E. Hutton general partner, to celebrate W. E. Hutton & Company's entry into the commodity futures trading field. The New York–based company's membership stirred celebration for the seat's $100,000 price tag, at that time the highest in the history of U.S. commodity exchange firms.

CME not only explored the range of opportunities available to the IMM, but also moved ahead with an ambitious plan to educate and inform corporate America on the value of using the currency markets, specifically the IMM. In its initial stages, CME published a wealth of information and statistics on the use of foreign exchange while offering lectures, study courses, symposia, and conferences.[10] As the financial world continued to move at a hectic pace, however, CME could not afford to wait for major corporations to see the value in the IMM. The exchange had to consistently search for ways to move ahead. Soon, the next logical step arrived—gold. Robert Abboud, who at the time headed the International Department at the First National Bank of Chicago, said:

The thing the traders want most of all is to be able to make money, and if you've got a product that is successful, and you're able to make money, then the resistance melts away.

The first big thing was the establishment of the IMM. Once you got that in and you began to have contracts, and you began to have volumes, then you draw in the major institutions around the country and around the world as participants, and you begin

adding products, and each successive product is challenged. [The IMM and its success] added a whole range of complexity. So none of these things are easy. Each one has its own dynamics. But you've got a track record of success in the other products, and therefore, your acceptance level increases.[11]

Melamed journeyed to London, the world's only city with an established gold market, and researched the possibility of trading futures contracts in gold on the CME floor. On January 1, 1975, Americans would be allowed to own gold contracts, and a subsequent battle for the futures contracts among the nation's exchanges would undoubtedly arise. Melamed's trek to London sparked a surefire way that CME could beat other exchanges hoping to enter the gold market as well.

By the fall of 1973, CME's new Jackson Boulevard home was already a swirl of traders donning colored jackets and booming voices. Embracing its intense growth, CME readied plans for expansion of the new facility.

"If we could [establish a gold fix on the IMM floor immediately], then by the time it was legal for futures trading in gold, the IMM would have the upper hand," said Melamed. "It was a guaranteed route to beat everyone in the gold derby."[12]

In August 1974, Melamed met with U.S. Treasury Department representatives and urged the Treasury to allow futures contracts in gold. Melamed cautioned the government that foreign speculators could purchase gold abroad and later sell it to Americans at higher prices. A futures market in gold, said Melamed, could help stabilize the situation.

Finally, on December 31, 1974, CME bestowed its gold contract on the IMM, allowing American citizens to own gold contracts for the first time in the nation's history.[13] The IMM wasn't alone, however, as gold contracts also opened on trading floors at COMEX in New York and on the Chicago Board of Trade (CBOT). COMEX, with an established reputation for trading in metals, was the clear favorite as the CBOT soon became a minor player in the gold trading game. Left alone to battle COMEX for supremacy, Melamed urged the IMM traders

to stick with the fight, pledging that their invest-ment and trust in CME would prove worthwhile.

Enter the CFTC

With the impact of Watergate (the nation's largest political scandal) still resonating through-out the land, U.S. congressmen prowled about the Capital with reform on the mind. Long a curiosity of the government and even the general public, futures trading emerged as a likely target. In fact, the futures industry drew the significant ire of both consumers and U.S. farmers, parties insistent that exchange traders were responsible for skyrocketing prices on a range of agricultural commodities. Melamed was just one of many contending that the futures markets were little more than messengers in the process, alerting others of what stands around the corner, but clearly never defining the prices.

"[The 1970s] was a period where the industry had to respond to some major image challenges. This had been a fundamentally unregulated indus-try for a long period of time," said Clayton K. Yeutter,

In August 1974, President Gerald Ford repealed the four-decade-old ban on gold contracts in the United States. By December 31, 1974, CME had its gold contract up and running with nearly 800 contracts traded on the first day.

who assumed the CME presidency in 1978. "This was sort of the last frontier of traders conduct-ing themselves basically as they wished. It wasn't really the law of the jungle, but it was a situation where if there were corrections taken for improper conduct, it was usually corrections taken by mem-bers themselves."[14]

In early 1974, the House Agricultural Committee introduced the Commodity Futures Trading Com-mission Act, thereby establishing the framework for a governmental regulatory agency for the futures industry. Beginning in April 1974, the Commodity Futures Trading Commission (CFTC)—a name determined by a coin flip among congressmen—would replace the Commodity Exchange Authority, the contract markets' governmental watchdog since

1936, and one that came under fire for its perceived lack of enforcement during the early 1970s. CME's lobbying, coupled with that of other U.S. futures exchanges, could do little to reverse the tide of reform.

"[The futures exchanges] were all against it. They had self-regulating mechanisms in place, and they didn't see a need for it. Commodity futures trading is a very consensual situation," said Beverly Splane, who worked in the Ford White House and led the CFTC's search for a chairman and commissioners.[15] Yet, rather than passively observe the creation of its new regulatory agency, CME led other exchanges in active participation.

Modeling its relationship to the futures industry as the Security and Exchange Commission was to stocks, the CFTC's reach expanded from the world of agricultural commodities, the historical emperor of the exchanges, to the novel arena of financial instruments. While some worried about excessive governmental oversight, others, including Melamed and some of his CME colleagues, maintained a more positive outlook. Perhaps, they reasoned, benefits could be gleaned from a governmental agency—credibility, the potential removal of physical delivery, and the ability of the oversight agency to act as a middle man between the futures industry and its critics.

With the retirement of CME executive vice president Kenneth Mackay, who had been with CME for nearly five full decades, exchange hierarchy began searching for a replacement. Throughout the process of helping to shape the CFTC, CME leaders became acquainted with Splane, the CFTC's active executive director. Melamed, who earlier had resisted Splane's overture that he head the CFTC, offered Splane the post vacated by Mackay. She accepted and, in doing so, became the first woman executive vice president of any U.S. exchange.[16]

Around the same time as Splane's appointment in 1975, Mark Powers left for a new position in the nation's capital. The man who had helped shape the IMM alongside Melamed and Everette B. Harris was leaving to serve as the CFTC's chief economist.

In a Word: Unity

As the decade of the 1970s pushed onward, CME's future became clear, although its present remained clouded with discontent. CME's rapid success led to rising hostility with some members, most often sparked by animosity between the two sister exchanges as well as the shared space, much of which the IMM had taken over at Jackson Boulevard. Melamed said:

Agriculture was never going to be the future. But finance was. If Chicago Mercantile Exchange had any future, it was on the back of the International Monetary Market. But that was something I couldn't prove in 1975, because the currencies and financial futures still had a long way to go. One had to believe. And at the moment, the agricultural markets were still on top and in a boom.[17]

CME President Everette B. Harris agreed with Melamed's assessment. Concerned about the health of both exchanges, CME leaders created a special committee in 1975 to explore solutions. Within a few months, the committee presented its findings. The chief proposal was for CME to bring in more

Left: With only two years of existence to its credit, the IMM continued to forge ahead with new products. In 1974, CME President Everette B. Harris (left) joined trader Phillip Glass to observe the opening of the division's French Franc futures contract.

Opposite: The sounds of progress. CME President Everette B. Harris sounded a copper bell to signal the opening of the copper contract on July 1, 1974.

members to keep its markets viable and liquid. Above all, however, the committee preached unity, a shared spirit that had helped CME ward off disasters in the past.

"It was a unique force of unity, of purpose by our members, which enabled CME to innovate, to explore, to brazenly promote our ideas, and in the end, to succeed," the committee's report said. Acknowledging the growing division between the respective exchanges, the committee urged CME to prevent a greater schism at all costs.[18]

Taking the committee's findings to heart, the Boards of each exchange soon reasoned that a unified exchange would be a stronger exchange. A potential merger plan circulated among leaders of both CME and the IMM with conflicting voices demanding to be heard. Although CME was the parent exchange and the de facto leader, it nevertheless had little say

In 1975, CME and the IMM merged to create one institution. Before the merger, the two exchanges existed side by side on the trading floor while conducting separate activities.

in IMM matters. The financial exchange, however, understood its unique position. The IMM represented the future of the industry and CME. While the IMM may have held substantial promise, CME maintained the benefits of its connections, finance, and years of an established base. Melamed explained:

The IMM couldn't exist without the CME infrastructure. How could we? We didn't have any money yet. If this thing was going to be built as the giant I thought it would be, it had to depend on the Chicago Mercantile Exchange for board markers,

IN THE AGRICULTURAL PITS

IN THE BEGINNING WAS THE WORD. A trader's word. Veteran agricultural trader Steve Newcom says the word is all one has in the pits, especially amid CME's most intense agricultural trading days. "In the older days, so much of it was built upon trust. You made a trade with someone. The old saying that your word was your bond, that was really true," said Newcom.

A native of central Indiana and its seemingly endless row of farms, Steve Newcom arrived at CME in 1977 with a résumé boasting of degrees in agricultural economics (a bachelor's degree from Purdue University and a master's degree from the University of Missouri) and experience in the agricultural markets from early career work at Continental Bank. He soon after purchased a membership for $160,000 and ventured into CME's agricultural trading pits, a world unique unto itself with many of the exchange's storied personalities and old guard names dominating the pits' actions.

At CME in the mid-1970s, raw commodities—pork bellies, live cattle, and hogs—still commanded CME business, while financial futures, launched in 1972, remained a growing phenomenon with overwhelming potential. Through embargos, inflation, deflation, and the immense rise of financial instruments, CME's agricultural section, the roots of the exchange, has maintained its viability and purpose amid changing times.

Agricultural products and their traders, such as Newcom, retain their place among the CME's diverse product line. Newcom says the basics of trading and the market remain the same today as they did three decades ago, during his first days at the exchange. He explained:

It's a testament to the viability of our markets and, if you give them time, how well they are capable of sorting everything out. It's proven to us that if you try to manipulate or restrict either a supply side or demand side, you throw the equation way out of whack. If you allow the industry itself to handle anything that's thrown askew for a moment, it will right itself in a shorter period of time than if you try to do it with any kind of political or fiscal instruments, and I think we've proven that over time.

The agricultural pits are no less active and intense today than during Newcom's early days, particularly since CME stands as the nation's only active market on livestock commodities from pork bellies to hogs and feeder cattle. "As far as people in the pit, it is still quite active," he said. "In fact, our open interest is at record levels, which is significant. But of course, the whole industry is growing so rapidly our percentage hasn't changed."[1]

for administrative help, for all of the things that CME allowed.

There's a political, horrible landmine. So I started to think that the only thing to do was to merge the two institutions. Let's come back to the Chicago Mercantile Exchange, our mother, then we're all one.[19]

On October 6, 1975, CME and IMM Boards approved the proposed merger and reorganization of the two institutions. With the Boards in agree-

ment, the focus now turned to each institution's respective membership—parties experiencing the growing hostility firsthand on the Jackson Boulevard trading floor. Some members, like young trader Bill Shepard, were easy converts.

"I always viewed what was good for one was good for the other. What was good for the institution was good for both," said Shepard, who, like many others, claimed ownership stakes in both CME and IMM. "I never looked at it as us versus them."[20]

Other members, meanwhile, old butter and egg stalwarts coupled with non-IMM seat-holders, as well as the singular IMM traders, would prove more difficult to sell on the merger plan. On November 2, 1975, one day before the proposal would arrive at a membership vote, an open meeting took place at the downtown Bismarck Hotel. One by one, the standing-room–only crowd voiced their concerns to exchange leaders. Though recognizing the difficulty of the challenge at hand, Melamed was not alone in recognizing the need to honor the democratic spirit CME had long held so tight.

"The member's question was being addressed … in an open forum where all the members could hear the spontaneity of the answer, judge the honesty of the response, and have the ability to follow up immediately with another question," Melamed said. "In other words, a members' meeting allowed debate, the lifeblood of a democracy, and of an exchange."[21]

Although the members-only meeting was not without its share of tension—loyalists from each side voicing their discontent—it was apparent to most in attendance that the merger served a sound purpose. The following day, November 3, 1975, CME members voted 343 to 23 in favor of the plan, while the IMM approved it 396 to 57.[22] Thereafter, the IMM became a division of CME, the surviving institution, while another division, the Non-Livestock Market (later renamed the Associate Mercantile Market Division), was created to spur trading in some of CME's overlooked markets—eggs, lumber, milo (a drought-resistant sorghum) butter, and frozen turkeys.[23] IMM members were limited to trading in financial markets alone, while CME members claimed access to all markets. In January 1976, as the merger settled into place, Melamed was elected as the first chairman of the unified CME, a position he sought for the ability to fashion a future path for the promising institution.

"Although, to my knowledge, [the merger] proposed had never before been attempted at any exchange, I felt certain that it would work," said Melamed, giving a nod to CME's belief in the free market spirit as well as the exchange's capabilities.[24]

Unity Demands More Space

The need for additional space to accommodate the swelling amount of traders working the pits proved one of the many contentious points among traders in the pre-merger days. When CME leaders planned the move from Franklin Street to Jackson Boulevard, they understood they would gain much-needed space; they did not, however, accurately anticipate the immense growth that would occur at the exchange within a matter of years. Melamed recalled:

In 1970, when we instituted the plans for our new quarters at 444 West Jackson, nobody had financial futures in mind. When we moved in 1972, the IMM had already been born, an infant of six months. A scant four years later, the successful new IMM contracts were pushing us against the wall. Not only didn't we have enough room to launch any of the new markets we had on the drawing boards, we could hardly manage existing business. It brought us to the embarrassing conclusion, albeit one made with some perverse pride, that we had no choice but to either move again or expand the new premises.[25]

Amid the CME–IMM merger talks, plans for an expansion of the already outgrown Jackson Boulevard home also took precedence. With the Chicago River flowing along the building's east side, expansion potential was limited. Returning to the architectural firm of Skidmore, Owings & Merrill, LLP, the eventual plan for expansion called for the building to be extended 90 feet west. The proposal, however, needed approval from the city and, most notably, its ironfisted mayor, Richard J. Daley. CME would need to purchase air rights from the city to extend the structure over the Canal Street sidewalk, an idea approved only once in the city's history.[26]

Melamed arrived at the mayor's fifth-floor city hall office in the summer of 1975 armed with the architectural plans and a diverse set of pleas. With consideration, Daley listened to CME's pitch and, upon Melamed's completion, asked a simple question: "What will it do for Chicago?"

Briefly taken aback by the question, Melamed responded, "Mr. Mayor, if I am right about financial futures, the IMM will move the center of financial gravity of this country a couple of miles westward from New York."[27]

That answer appeased Daley enough, and he granted his approval for CME's expansion, one that would nearly double the available trading floor space.

Additionally, the expansion allowed traders in the pits to stretch their arms while also affording CME added space to unveil the latest in financial contracts.

Get Your T-bills!

With a new organizational structure, growing harmony, added space, and the promise of the future all gracing the exchange, a new contract was added to the trading boards on January 6, 1976—the 90-day U.S. Treasury bill futures contract.

Prior to leaving for a position with the CFTC, Mark Powers had convinced CME leaders that the

In 1978, the CME presidency passed from Everette B. Harris to Clayton K. Yeutter, shown here addressing Wyoming cattlemen in 1978. Yeutter, a Nebraskan farm native, boasted a résumé filled with law achievements, government appointments, and political experience.

90-day T-bill contract could become a valuable instrument in a financial world increasingly gravitating toward short-term monetary instruments. After navigating the political waters and securing government approval, CME, true to form, created a T-bill Specifications Committee that included Melvin Unterman, Philip Glass, William Goldstandt, and Atlee Kohl. Unterman arrived at the idea of applying the IMM index to the T-bill contract.[28] CME leaders, however, further understood that merely posting the contract would not attract business; rather, the exchange had to sell the T-bill futures contract and its value to the financial community.

"Each futures product had to carry its own weight no matter how successful the exchange was as an entity," Melamed said. "Just as the idea of currency futures had to be sold to banks, the idea of T-bill futures had to be sold to investment bankers."[29]

CME then targeted some of the nation's largest investment banking firms, including New York heavyweight Salomon Brothers. The wait-and-see approach of senior partner William Salomon represented a typical response.[30] With the T-bill tied to inflation and interest rates, many investment banking institutions were content to delay any full-fledged support of the contract, though most also acknowledged that its success would quickly bring their entrance into the market.

On the morning of January 6, 1976, when CME ally and Nobel Laureate Milton Friedman, PhD, rang the opening bell to commence trading in T-bills, an outbreak of activity ensued. Within the first five minutes, 105 T-bill contracts were traded, a sign that CME had indeed pushed the right button.[31]

"T-bills became one of those rare futures instruments, an instant success," conceded Melamed.

A Pivotal Moment

Though not among the first drafts of currencies the IMM would trade, the Mexican peso nevertheless made its way to the trading floor as one of the original seven foreign currencies when the IMM opened in 1972. Four years later, on August 31, 1976, the Mexican peso would help alter the world's outside view of the IMM. As the world's only market trading the peso, the IMM was the benefactor of Mexico's decision to devalue their currency by 50

JACK SANDNER'S RISE

THROUGHOUT ITS HISTORY, CME HAS hosted a variety of pit traders and a range of institutional leaders with remarkable stories. These stories depict the nation's idealistic lore in action. John F. "Jack" Sandner's story, however, rivals them all.

A native Chicagoan from the city's south side, Sandner proved an excellent student and athlete during his years in a Catholic grammar school. A quick study, Sandner was the first to learn Latin in his class, and the only fourth grader to serve as an altar boy for midnight mass on Christmas Eve. At the age of 15, Sandner was the youngest contestant to ever win the rock 'n' roll dance contest where he performed to a sold-out crowd at the Chicago Harvest Moon Festival held in Chicago Stadium.

During Sandner's high school years, his world began to fall apart. His father succumbed to alcohol abuse and lost his job. As a result, his mother, an orphan from the Bridgeport neighborhood in Chicago, took on two jobs to support the family. Sandner had to change high schools in order to attend one closer to home—Chicago Vocational— one of Chicago's most troubled high schools at the time. With South Chicago police officers as hall guards and race riots common occurrences, attending Chicago Vocational proved disastrous for young Sandner. At the end of his junior year, he dropped out of high school and took a job at the

Jack Sandner abandoned a successful career as a trial lawyer to trade in cattle, hogs, and pork bellies. His unrivaled 17-year reign as CME chairman started in 1980.

local gas station. With the second income, Sandner's mom could now quit one of her two jobs to take care of Sandner's father.

While working at the gas station, something happened that would ultimately change the course of Sandner's life. His gas station buddies entered him into a boxing tournament. After Sandner's first fight, Tony Zale, the former middleweight world champion, approached him to unlace his gloves. He offered to teach Sandner how to fight. Jack was in awe. He took Zale up on his offer and started fighting regularly. As Sandner began winning fights at athletic clubs,

percent.[32] The move sent reverberations throughout the financial community, and the IMM stood alone in quoting a price for the peso, and $96 million in contracts traded hands on the exchange floor.[33] Thanks to the peso, the IMM achieved the credibility it had long been seeking.

"It was a glorious and pivotal moment in IMM history. For the first time, the world of finance recognized the enormous value of the futures market," said Melamed, "The 1976 peso crisis proved to even the most stubborn doubters that a futures market

could provide a price for the world of hedgers and speculators under any circumstances."[34]

Melamed would later call the day "the critical turning point in IMM history."[35]

CME Goes to Washington

CME leaders, ever mindful that misconceptions of their business existed outside of the industry, consistently sought to educate and inform others on the legitimacy and necessity of the futures marthe Catholic Youth Organization, and local bars, college recruiters soon courted him. But without a high school diploma he was hamstrung.

Together, Zale and Sandner's mother convinced Jack that his mother could manage to make ends meet and take care of his father. They urged Sandner to return to high school. Having learned skills in the ring as well as the discipline he had lacked from Zale, Sandner returned to school and graduated valedictorian. As the commencement speaker for his class, he said, "Your future is not in the hands of fate, but in your desire and perseverance to make your own future."

With college boxing banned because of a fighter's death in 1960, Sandner transferred his energies to wrestling and study. He first attended the University of Arizona and later graduated from Southern Illinois University with a degree in psychology.[1] His English professor encouraged him to attend law school. Hesitantly, Sandner took the LSAT, but did not apply to law school. When the professor raised the idea of Sandner attending Notre Dame, Sandner flushed with excitement. He recalled playing the Notre Dame fight song on the piano in first grade. The deadline for application had already passed, but Sandner applied anyway. Not surprisingly, he was rejected.

Sandner, disappointed but not discouraged, drove to the South Bend campus and arrived at dawn. He waited on the steps of the law school building until Dean Joseph O'Meara arrived. Sandner pleaded his case, highlighting his rebirth, focus, and passion. He implored the dean to open the class for one more student. The dean listened to Sandner for a solid half-hour, then he said, "Your time is up. I have someone waiting." As Sandner rose to leave, the dean continued, "Mr. Sandner, be here August 22, ready for class." Three years later in 1968, Sandner graduated from Notre Dame Law School receiving the Dean's Award.[2] Engraved in bronze, his name hangs on the wall of the law school.

Sandner returned to Chicago as a trial lawyer, finding a place for his competitive nature. Through his legal work, Sandner met Everette B. Harris, the reigning CME president. Harris thought Sandner would be a good trader and urged Sandner to buy a seat. Harris guaranteed an $80,000 loan, and Sandner became a member. He would continue to practice law and trade at the noon hour in cattle, eggs, and pork bellies.[3] In 1975, he tried his last case. The day before, Sandner practiced his closing argument all night on an empty trading floor in the pork belly pit. He won the case and then became a full-time trader. Two years later, legendary trader Glenn Bromagen approached Sandner at the gym where Sandner worked out punching a body bag. He talked Sandner into running his commodities firm Rufenacht, Bromagen & Hertz, Inc.

At the same time, Bromagen encouraged Sandner to run for the CME Board. The nominating committee already had their slate set. Determined, Sandner ran on petition, and the membership overwhelmingly elected him. Two years later, he was elected vice chairman. In 1980, the Board unanimously elected Sandner chairman, setting the stage for an unprecedented reign that would span a period of 17 years. He became the longest-serving chairman in the history of the exchange.

kets. The U.S. government stood alone as the group requiring the most information. In the nation's capital, legislative leaders, those entrusted with the ability to shape and mold the nation's course in so many ways, remained lukewarm on the futures industry. For some lawmakers, the industry was an object of outright hostility. Throughout the years, the futures markets had indeed been a frequent source of criticism, the target of steady opposition amid charges of influencing the market. Complicating matters was the youth and mystery of the financial markets, an issue requiring added explanation. To combat misunderstandings in Washington, CME leaders again took the proactive road. If government leaders were to discover the value of the futures industry, the Merc, as it did during the formation of the CFTC, would be acknowledged to have played an enterprising role.

"Our new successes brought us national recognition; recognition brought us visibility; visibility made us political targets. And as targets we would be highly vulnerable without influence. The Merc needed influence if it was ever going to reach its potential and be a major player in the world financial markets," said Melamed.[36]

And in the United States, influence makes its home in Washington, D.C.

The impetus for the opening of CME's Washington office occurred in the winter of 1976 when CFTC Chairman Bill Bagley, at a meeting of CME members at the Bismarck Hotel, shared his shock regarding Washington's general ignorance of the futures industry.[37] CME Chairman Laurence Rosenberg led other exchange leaders in noting the need for a Washington presence, a weak point given CME's explosive growth in recent years. If continued progress were the goal, then CME would need to change its relationship with lawmakers and make the markets better understood. To CME leaders, that meant bringing Washington to Jackson Boulevard and allowing them to see the action of the pits, the center of the free marketplace. Yeutter said:

> *Futures trading had a dubious image at best in those days. It was looked upon by a lot of people as a gambling den and undeservedly so. A futures market provides a very valuable economic function in American society, but that was recognized by very few people anywhere except those participating in the industry. It certainly was not recognized on Capitol Hill.*
>
> *It was necessary to flip that image 180 degrees and say we want to welcome those folks from Washington, D.C., to come out and see what we're doing here. They needed to understand it and recognize that there's a valuable economic function being performed, and it's not just a gambling den. So that was necessary.*[38]

Easier said than done. A mere invitation for lunch and a tour of the trading floor would surely yield but a few takers. CME needed an insider, a politically savvy, amiable guide to all things Washington to serve as the middle man. And the exchange found him in C. Dayle Henington, an administrative assistant and close friend of Representative W. R. Poage, the Texas chairman of the House Committee on Agriculture.[39] Henington proved instrumental in achieving

CME's objectives in Washington. He not only opened the exchange office at 1101 Connecticut Avenue in November 1978 but also successfully urged legislators to visit CME and see the markets for themselves, beginning with House Majority Leader Jim Wright.

The next step in CME's political maneuvering agenda again came from CFTC Chairman Bagley, who suggested that CME create a voice in Washington with political muscle and strength through a political action committee. Soon after, Melamed heeded Bagley's recommendation and established the Commodity Futures Political Fund (CFPF).[40] The CFPF would serve a necessary financial base to provide CME leaders with the opportunity to open the doors of communication with legislators in Washington. As a result, legislators came to visit Jackson Boulevard as well as the neighboring CBOT, an equal partner in the endeavor. Melamed frequently served as the voice for CME in Congress once Henington landed with the lawmakers at CME's door.

"My message to lawmakers was direct and cautionary: Chicago was the futures capital of the world," Melamed said. "Our exchanges had the foresight to change with the changes in the world. We had the guts to be innovative. And, as a consequence, we brought world business to Chicago. But we were more than that. Our markets were an integral part of the financial services arena of our country."[41]

And with that, CME made friends in Washington, a necessary alliance to benefit its growth in the years to come.

"Part of the good work that was done [by CME] was the fact that they established a lot of trust with members of Congress—that what they were telling them was direct, honest, not spinning them," said Dan Glickman, a congressman and former secretary of agriculture, who got to know CME well during his 18 years in Washington. "The Chicago exchanges were among the leaders building these relationships, personal relationships, with Capitol Hill members."[42]

Despite the focus on Washington, CME leaders still maintained an attentive eye on the health of the exchange, monitoring its progress and exploring the institution's future path. The movement in Washington, exchange leaders con-

THE FREE MARKET SPIRIT IN ACTION

IN 1980, THE SOVIET UNION INVADED Afghanistan, prompting U.S. President Jimmy Carter, whom later would boycott the 1980 Summer Olympics in Moscow as a protest, to order an embargo on the sale of $2.6 billion in corn, wheat, and soybeans.[1] The embargo dealt a dizzying blow to the nation's grain market. Subsequently, the CFTC suspended grain trading at the CBOT. CME, ever the champion of the "free markets for free men" spirit, immediately sparked dialogue to the defense of free markets.

CME Chairman Jack Sandner, whom only months before assumed the leading role, emerged the voice of the exchange and became an unlikely ally to CFTC Chairman James Stone. Following the CFTC's suspension of grain trading at the CBOT, Sandner and Stone met in Washington, with Stone reminding Sandner that the halt to trading at the CBOT was little of his or CME's business. Sandner, the gritty south sider with a penchant for returning sturdy blows, soon after penned a letter to Stone in which he firmly stated, "An attack on free enterprise no matter where it takes place is an attack on us."[2]

Sandner's aggressive and quick defense would set the course for CME's active role as an outspoken leader for not only the free market system but also the business of exchanges throughout the country. For so long, others, including the nation's government, peered at the futures industry with a skeptical glare. Neither Sandner nor CME wished to maintain a reserved posture against regulatory intervention and questions of effective self-regulation.

With a spirit resembling both its city and its leaders—past and present—CME defended the free enterprise ideals with vigor and purpose.

In the middle of the trading pit, Jack Sandner bought and sold. Living by his mantra—free markets for free men— Sandner wore his message embroidered on his trading jacket.

tended, was not to distract from the current and future progress of CME.

"The primary efforts of our leadership," said Melamed, "had to be focused on growth, momentum, new markets, and innovation. Our political and cultural activities were to be used only to enhance the potential of our underlying objectives."[43]

The End of an Era

In November 1978, the same month of CME's Washington office opening, the exchange endured a passing of the torch with the appointment of Clayton K. Yeutter as CME's new president, only the second in exchange history. A year earlier, CME President Everette B. Harris, whom had been at the helm of the exchange for a wild 25-year ride that included the near death of the exchange as well as the creation of the IMM, floated the idea of retirement. The beloved Harris, a fixture of CME's spirit with his gregarious nature, soon settled upon 1978 as his final year. He would then help CME find his successor, one that would represent CME's shifting image from that of a local player to that of a global leader.

"The IMM was the international key, the bridge to London, Tokyo, Singapore, Hong Kong, Frankfurt, and Paris," said Melamed, whose decade of leadership with Harris produced some of the exchange's most fruitful results. "[CME] needed someone not only with Washington contacts but who could move in international circles as well. We were projecting a new and different image."[44]

In 1977, as Melamed's second reign as chairman came to a close, the CME Board of Directors created a special counsel to the Board post to which Melamed was appointed and from which he continued to lead the institution. Melamed remained in this appointed post until 1985, when his leadership role was again formalized with his appointment as chairman of the executive com-

mitee, an office he held until his temporary retirement in 1990.

The Board's initial plan was to bring in a new president from the outside, and the group soon discovered Clayton K. Yeutter as the ideal fit. Despite reservations about CME, coupled with his own political ambitions, Yeutter, a polished man with roots in agriculture, law, and government, accepted the post.

More important to CME personnel, however, was Yeutter's ability to tap into his political contacts with an outgoing nature and free-market soul. Yeutter defined his role in the CME structure by saying he would play an active role in the nation's capital because "that's where the action is."[45] Given his stated objective, Yeutter then responded by activating an ambitious travel plan throughout the nation and overseas. Moving from one city to the next, Yeutter touted the benefits of CME markets, while the traders on Jackson Boulevard continued to build CME business.

"The CME had established the Washington, D.C., office just before I came, but they really didn't know what to do with it. So what I brought them was a broader experience base of Washington and the world, and got them started on a track of seeing themselves as much more than just a sleepy Chicago exchange," said Yeutter.[46]

In January 1980, CME became the first American exchange to open a London office. With the help of Kimberly Albright, an American working for Citibank's London office until hired by CME's Beverly Splane, CME found an overseas office in the heart of London's financial district at 27 Throgmorton Street.

In 1980, retired CME President Everette B. Harris (seated, center) found himself surrounded by a host of CME chairmen at a banquet honoring the longtime chief's work at the exchange. Sitting (left to right): Michael J. Weinberg, Jr.; Nathan A. Wertheimer; Harris; Michael Weinberg, Sr.; and William S. Katz. Standing (left to right): John T. Geldermann; Laurence M. Rosenberg; John F. "Jack" Sandner; Leo Melamed; Stephen Greenberg; and Robert J. O'Brien.

Jack and London

Following the opening of its Washington office, CME soon turned its sights elsewhere to the east—all the way across the Atlantic. Europe claimed no futures exchanges and, subsequently, hedging and a currency market failed to take hold. Although London possessed an active gold market joined by an options market in metals, there was little else in the way of something even loosely resembling CME. That alone made London a logical choice for CME's first foreign office.

In early 1979, CME began to plan the opening of a London office to capitalize on the tremendous European potential in financial futures trading. In addition, the success of the 90-day T-bill contract launched in 1976 alongside the one-year T-bill (opened September 11, 1978), and four-year Treasury note contracts (opened July 10, 1979), furthered CME's contention that financial instruments lined the impending course of the futures industry.

In January 1980, a 38-year-old named Jack Sandner assumed the chairmanship at CME. A scrappy former boxer with a quick right hook and an even quicker spirit, Sandner typified CME's evolving image as a place of innovation, guts, and hustle. And he had just inherited the reins of the world's second-largest futures exchange. Sandner, however, also took over an exchange desiring to expand its global influence, yet needing to refine its overseas image. Sandner discovered the latter from Leo Melamed, whose own trek to London proved an eye-opener on the image battles CME would face abroad.

Eager to establish a European presence, as well as continue an active gold market battling New York's COMEX, CME officials readied plans to turn the ideas of a London office into reality. As other U.S.–based financial institutions such as Merrill Lynch and Thompson McKinnon were establishing a European presence, CME understood the time had come for its arrival as well.

But first the exchange had to find a location, as well as someone to head the office—someone British and someone familiar with the financial markets.[47] In Keith Woodbridge, a 26-year veteran of Citibank, CME had found its man for the job. Soon after, Kimberly Albright, previously hired by Beverly Splane to find CME a London space, discovered CME's home at 27 Throgmorton Street in the heart of the city's financial district. As such, CME became the first U.S. exchange to open a London office.[48] And true to historical form, CME educated the London public on the markets. Although a challenging sell to the British, CME stood committed to the endeavor and pledged its full support to the move. In a black-tie affair at London's Guild Hall, Sandner toasted to Queen Elizabeth, a symbol of just how far CME had come.

In less than a decade, and with the Reagan era approaching, CME had not only launched the revolutionary IMM but also moved to modernize its headquarters, expanded that space, opened contracts in T-bills and gold, and found a new president, while witnessing the departure of an institutional legend, and created offices in Washington, D.C., and London. Perhaps as active a decade as any in its history, CME's momentum pushed forward like never before. But rarely in its history has CME, Chicago's underdog, been content and passive. The futures industry could endure more growth, and CME would propel the process forward.

By the early 1980s, CME's financial trading pits on Jackson Boulevard had become a crowded and active marketplace, one highlighted by the certificate of deposit futures contract and the Eurodollar futures contract.

CHAPTER SIX

CME BECOMES A GLOBAL PLAYER

1981–1984

Bring people to the field of dreams, and they will trade, and ... you want them to trade because you want liquidity so you can get in and out of the market. Liquidity is the name of the game. Real estate—it's location, location, location. In futures and trading—liquidity, liquidity, liquidity.

—Jack Sandner

WITH RONALD REAGAN in the White House and the 1980s under way, Chicago Mercantile Exchange (CME) assumed its spot among the world's elite futures exchanges. The 1970s had proved to be a decade of immense growth, prosperity, and credibility. The trading of the ultimate commodity—money—had paved the way for CME leaders who aggressively pursued innovative new markets with a renewed spirit and vitality. For all of its growth, however, CME refused to rest. Trading in money opened new avenues for CME, and the exchange stood determined to capture all that was possible.

In 1980, trading volume in gold, foreign currency, and T-bill futures, for the first time in CME's history, had overtaken the agricultural products.[1] Membership at the exchange grew to more than 1,300, while trading volume rose to an all-time high of 23 million contracts, valued at $23-billion notional on a daily basis. The number of contracts had also expanded to 20, ranging from financial instruments to the popular pork bellies, a distant cry from less than 20 years earlier, when CME placed its livelihood in a basket of eggs after the government ban on onion trading.[2] In fact, the certificate of deposit (CD) contract, which opened on July 29, 1981, signaled CME's largest opening day, when more than 4,200 con-

tracts changed hands. CME continued on the fast track. With the CD contract, CME furthered its mission of providing unique risk-management tools to a range of clients throughout the business world.

The Eurodollar

If anyone had earned the right to stand and shout about new contracts for CME, it was Leo Melamed. The architect behind the exchange's financial futures initiatives, Melamed, who had earned a national—if not global—reputation for his work with the International Monetary Market (IMM), looked elsewhere to discover CME's next pioneering contract. And he found it overseas.

"At that time, I was digging into interest rates. I realized that the ultimate contract out there—not the ultimate contract because that's stock index futures—but in a sense, the ultimate short-term interest rate contract was the interest rate on dollars traded in the world. There was this huge overhanging of dollars ... in banks, deposits, all over the world," Melamed said.

Despite all the attention given to financial contracts, CME's agricultural pits continued as active marketplaces as well.

"From all my studies, I realized that if you could measure the interest rate movement of the dollars in Europe ... in other words, Eurodollars ... that interest rate quotient was the most important benchmark for the short term, even more important than Treasury bills because it was everywhere, and it was what everyone saluted. Treasury bills were peculiarly an American interest rate, whereas Eurodollars were a world interest rate thought factor."[3]

Only one problem emerged: Cash settlement of futures contracts was a concept not yet at work in the United States. T-bills and CDs could be delivered; but they were physically delivered instruments. Eurodollars, however, were something else. The mere idea of delivery, an act that occurred in less than two percent of all contracts traded, allowed the futures industry in the United States to separate itself from the undesirable gambling label. As the rate of interest, Eurodollars were intangible. Traders would only want the difference in value from when they bought and when they sold the contract, and cash would be the preferred method of payment. Complicating matters further was the fact that each bank claimed a different interest rate; no standard formula or number survived. Melamed said:

No one really wants the product traded. The product is delivered two percent of the time.

You want the insurance factor that product price represents. Even if you buy cattle, you don't buy cattle to get delivery through the Chicago Mercantile Exchange.

If you did cash settlement and were allowed to do cash settlement, then you would need an index that everyone saluted; in fact, the price that everyone agreed to was the correct price at the time of maturity. Instead of delivery, everyone would salute the price—the equivalent.[4]

Hotly debated among the U.S. government's regulatory agencies, as well as the nation's exchanges, cash settlement would eventually open another door for the modern futures market. Though Australia's Sydney Futures Exchange (SFE) launched its own cash-settled futures contract in 1980, the idea in the United States, first proposed in 1977, stalled amid controversy and curiosity.[5] CME urged governmental approval, pointing to the fact that the futures exchanges never intended to provide physical delivery.

CME chief economist Fred Arditti journeyed to London in anticipation of the Commodity Futures Trading Commission's (CFTC) approval of the exchange's Eurodollars contract, a sign that CME stood confident regarding cash settlement's place in the futures arena. After several weeks abroad, making calls on global banks, Arditti returned and drafted the specifications for the Eurodollar contract and, more specifically, the IMM index, a challenging task that turned cash settlement from theory into black-and-white reality.

"It was so letter perfect. No one questioned its validity. No one questioned that it was a fair and honest determination of short-term interest rates for dollars anywhere in Europe, anywhere in the world, and this is the beauty of what Fred Arditti did," Melamed said. "It was the ability to put together from all the banks and commercial entities, an index that would represent short-term interest rates. To this day, it created the con-

CME President Clayton K. Yeutter (center) would help lead the exchange at a critical time in history. His credibility with lawmakers and his political know-how helped CME gain a voice in Washington.

Above: CME Chairman Jack Sandner (left), CME President Clayton K. Yeutter (center), and CME Special Counsel Leo Melamed (right) participated in a transatlantic press conference to commemorate the launch of the Eurodollar contract.

Right: Chairman Jack Sandner sounded the bell to signal the launch of the Eurodollar contract. In the coming years, the Eurodollar would gain the reputation as the world's most actively traded interest rate contract.

tract that is the biggest and most actively traded in the world."[6]

He added, "It was so good, it was so right, from day one, [that] the IMM index ... became the bell-wether of the world for interest rate futures."[7]

CME's well-tuned arguments directed at the government, along with Arditti's IMM index, yielded the desired results as the CFTC approved the exchange's proposal for a contract on three-month Eurodollar time deposits.[8] Cash settlement simplified the process and alleviated the burdening process of setting up bank accounts and other red tape; it would prove to be a monumental step for both CME and the financial world.

On December 19, 1981, CME unveiled Eurodollar futures, thereby establishing yet another revolutionary concept in the futures industry with the first cash-settled contract. On that day, CME Chairman Jack Sandner, Leo Melamed, and CME President Clayton K. Yeutter held a transatlantic press conference to London to underscore that the Eurodollar contract was not CME's alone—it was the world's contract.

Although CME anticipated that the majority of Eurodollar business eventually would arrive from outside the United States, CME still understood the need to encourage the traders on Jackson Boulevard to venture into the Eurodollar pits.[9]

Above all else, however, CME recognized the box it had opened. Cash settlement, as pioneered by CME's Eurodollar contract, would lead to new innovations throughout the 1980s and beyond, including CME's entry into the stock index arena.

Author and CME historian Bob Tamarkin would later comment, "Cash settlement was the biggest innovation since the introduction of currencies in 1972 because it opened the way for the cash-settled stock indices, the futures product that would dominate the 1980s."[10]

The Ultimate Contract

Turning back the clock almost 30 years, a charismatic trader, well-known on the floor, had edged up next to Leo Melamed, then an unknown runner working for Merrill Lynch while attending law school. Elmer Falker, a veteran of the exchange with a visionary's mind, grabbed Melamed's arm and prophesied that the ultimate industry contract was in stock market futures. Melamed's eyes lit up with curiosity, and he asked Falker why no one had ever attempted the task. "You can't make delivery," Falker said.[11]

And with that Melamed not only had his answer but also a piqued interest that would percolate in

The explosive growth of CME often demanded that the exchange evolve on the run. In 1981, it merged the past with the present in the pits, as automated boards with digital numbers joined the old manual blackboards covered in chalk dust.

After identifying the problems, Sandner and Melamed considered solutions. Asking the veteran traders to leave their traditional markets for the upstart S&P was a tricky proposition. But asking them to merely give just a fraction of their trading day to the S&P pit might be a way to stabilize and add to the S&P's fortunes. Sandner and Melamed then conceived the "15 Minutes Please" campaign, which urged CME's more seasoned traders to merely give the S&P pit 15 minutes of their daily trading time and thereby advance the market's liquidity.[16]

Sandner explained, "I stood there for three days ... handing out buttons. Fifteen minutes, please. You go in, take some risks. Spread. You'll have less risk spreading than taking naked posi-

S&P 500 INDEX SOARS

O N APRIL 21, 1982, CME OPENED ITS S&P 500 index and achieved the most active opening of any contract in the industry's history. Nearly 30,000 contracts changed hands in April's final days alone, while the exchange experienced record volume in seven of the year's nine remaining months. In a 1982 speech to members, CME Chairman Jack Sandner said:

We at the CME have built a cathedral to free enterprise. We are determined people; we are aggressive people. We are doers; we are originators. We are a mixture of formally educated and practically experienced people. We are planners. We capitalize on change. We are challengers; we are interested in the past only as a prelude to the future. We are opinionated, sometimes stubborn. We think pragmatically and are very profit-oriented. We thrive on competition. That's how I think of us. That's why nothing we accomplish will surprise me.[1]

tions, but go in there so that the institutions we're trying to have trade can get in and out of the market. You are a liquidity provider. That's what you do. Go in and do it, but only do it for 15 minutes."[17] Melamed remembers it equally as well:

All of our members were busy everywhere. They were in Eurodollars, in Treasury bills, in currencies—and currencies were in seven different markets. ... [We] thought, "They won't refuse us 15 minutes." [Jack Sandner and I] came in early before any member on the floor and ... we were standing at that door. ... [We] gave them a button, and we said, "Listen, just give us 15 minutes a day. Trade this S&P contract." I used to have guys come up to me after they traded, hand me their cards and say, "Leo, I was there 15 minutes. See, these are my trades. Look at the time."

Almost within days, you could see the volume shift. ... Within a month after that program, I knew we had won. The first mover, the guy with the volume, the guy with the liquidity, wins the deal. And the traders were hooked. ... Once they got the bicycle going, got the feel for the market, they were there.[18]

Indeed, within one month, conditions in the S&P pit had not only stabilized but prospered. By the end of 1982, CME's volume had ballooned to more than 24.5 million contracts, marking the fifth consecutive year of record activity.

The next move, on January 28, 1983, was to open trading in CME's S&P 500 options contract. As a risk-management business, CME now possessed the ability to offer clients a hedging instrument against stock market risk, while also allowing others to gain access to the stock market without owning shares.[19] The release of the options contract was but one more way in which CME would solidify its stature as one of the world's most progressive and active futures markets.

To Wacker Drive We Go

Throughout its recent history, CME had planned for expansion only to be overwhelmed by the sheer rate of its growth. When CME moved into new modernized headquarters on Jackson Boulevard in 1972, the institution allotted for 20 years of growth.[20] Within months, however, IMM trading volume pushed trading space to its limits, and by 1975, CME expanded its space by 30 percent to accommodate the swelling pits. By the early 1980s, CME began to pursue new quarters.

With trading in the pits reaching all-time highs, attention turned to CME's future home on Wacker Drive, between Madison and Monroe streets, just down the street from Chicago's famed Sears Tower. John Geldermann chaired CME's real estate committee and moved forward on the idea of creating a second trading floor to make way for future growth.[21] A portion of financing for the new building, $30 million in fact, arrived from CME's sale of IOM seats upon the release of the S&P 500 contract.[22] The building, referred to by some CME members as a "dream," as well as "the last piece to the puzzle," stood as a symbol of the exchange's remarkable evolution.

"By the time we were making plans for that new building, the exchange had really taken off," said CME President Clayton K. Yeutter. "People could see its prospects for the future. In other words, it wasn't just a pork belly and cattle exchange any more. There was a lot of enthusiasm in the Chicago community for the exchange."[23]

The $350-million plan, coordinated by the Levy Organization and designed by Fujikawa Johnson & Associates, called for granite to convey a significant architectural and institutional statement, "projecting the feel of security and strength,"

Melamed remarked.[24] The new CME would also provide 1 million square feet of office space in two parallel 40-story towers. In addition, a pair of trading floors tucked in between the rising towers, one 40,000 square feet and the other 30,000 square feet of column-free space, thereby providing CME with the title of the world's largest trading facility.[25]

When the facility opened its doors on November 28, 1983, nearly 11 years to the day of its Jackson Boulevard opening, CME celebrated with more than 100 guests, including representatives from the CFTC, the U.S. Congress, and the city. Chicago Mayor Harold Washington rang the opening bell, and Illinois Representative Dan Rostenkowski proudly proclaimed, "The Merc is to Chicago what oil is to Texas and Oklahoma, what milk is to Wisconsin, and what corn is to Iowa."[26]

CME, however, had not only become an important institution to its city, but in the process of its growth—both physically, with new modernized headquarters, as well as economically, with its progressive contracts—Chicago Mercantile Exchange had taken another step forward to becoming a dominant player in the global financial industry. Its focus remained forward-thinking and ahead of the rest.

An International Exchange

Sound leadership had carried CME to new heights throughout the 1970s and early 1980s. It began with the IMM and the revolutionary idea of trading in foreign currencies. With the Eurodollar, cash settlement, and the S&P 500 contract, the exchange gained additional momentum. Through it all, CME responded to countless challenges—from government regulators to eager competitors. The situation was no different in 1983, when the London International Financial Futures Exchange (LIFFE) placed CME in a precarious spot. LIFFE had opened in 1982 and modeled itself after CME. In fact, CME leaders were instrumental in helping

On August 12, 1981, CME broke ground for yet another move, this time to 20 South Wacker Drive, with visions of becoming the world's most modernized marketplace.

LIFFE take shape, even envisioning a potential linkup between the two exchanges sometime in the future. LIFFE posed a serious threat to CME's Eurodollar contract.

"Everyone in Chicago applauded. As the saying goes, imitation is the highest form of flattery," said Leo Melamed of LIFFE's opening. "In a very real sense, this was good for the futures. Competition is the fuel for success."[27]

Almost immediately, LIFFE's Eurodollar contract, a replica of CME's contract, began to take hold. Given the advantage of London's time zone, many European traders started turning to LIFFE for their risk-management needs, shunning CME's more established market.

"All other things being equal, futures market participants will use the market open during their business hours. This meant that as long as our two markets were more or less equal in product line, liquidity, and so forth, traders based in Europe would use LIFFE, while North American institutions would use the IMM," said Melamed.[28]

With LIFFE's continued emergence, gain in liquidity, and time-zone advantage, CME needed a response. Moreover, LIFFE's success, it was reasoned, might prompt others to duplicate the IMM blueprint. As the idea of a global economy became a reality, CME leaders rallied with vigor, inventiveness, and passion.

A partnership with an Asian exchange, CME leaders reasoned, would provide the necessary bridge to capitalize on the region's emerging market and untapped market participants, and allot CME a time-zone advantage all of its own. CME ruled out Hong Kong due to its divided atmosphere, and Japanese law prevented any potential relationship with Tokyo, the anticipated business capital of Asia. CME Chairman Brian Monieson, Leo Melamed, and Jack Sandner traveled to Singapore, encountering a group of eager and ambitious business-minded people. A half-world and 13 hours apart from its home base on Wacker Drive, CME found its Asian ally.

Leading the Singapore efforts was Lim Ho Kee, former chairman of the Singapore Gold Exchange, and Ng Kok Song, head of the Monetary Authority of Singapore. Both of them impressed CME leaders with their enthusiasm and optimism for the markets. A unique and unrivaled step, CME leaders

One of the many political leaders to visit the exchange over the years was Illinois Congressman Paul Simon (right), shown here with Leo Melamed in 1984. CME's open dialogue with government representatives served as a key ingredient in establishing its credibility on Capitol Hill.

determined that a partnership with Singapore would prove a worthy endeavor. CME's negotiating team of Monieson, Melamed, Sandner, Yeutter, CME Executive Vice President Bill Brodsky, CME Board members Barry Lind and Larry Rosenberg, and CME attorney Jerrold Salzman worked with the Singapore International Monetary Exchange (SIMEX) staff for three full days in Chicago. At the end of those three days, they completed details of an arrangement that would create an international link between the two institutions.[29]

One particularly contentious issue involved the creation of the Mutual Offset System (MOS), which would allow a trader to buy at one exchange and sell at another, thereby saving time and money. CME economist Michael Asay joined with colleague Roger Rutz and drafted the details of MOS.[30] In June 1984, a little more than a year after talks first began, the exchanges reached an official agreement, marking the first relationship of its type between an American futures exchange and an international counterpart. Beverly Splane, an integral CME leader in the linkage with SIMEX, explained:

TERRY DUFFY ENTERS THE PITS

LIKE MOST COLLEGE STUDENTS, TERRY Duffy had a summer job. He tended bar in Lake Geneva, Wisconsin, a resort town and frequent destination for many Chicagoans. A chance encounter in 1980, however, would forever alter the course of his life, one that would witness his rise from a runner on the exchange floor to eventual chairman of Chicago Mercantile Exchange.

In Lake Geneva, Duffy met Vince Schreiber, a well-known commodities trader at CME. Impressed by Duffy's mathematical mind, Schreiber encouraged Duffy to consider the commodities business. Ignorant of the industry, Duffy consistently shrugged off the overtures. Duffy frequently played midday golf with Schreiber, who invited him to an after-hours party at Schreiber's Frank Lloyd Wright–designed home on the lake. Schreiber's home, an expansive retreat filled with trading screens and pictures of Schreiber with influential figures, convinced Duffy to inquire further about the commodities business. So began the pair's mentor-protégé relationship, one that lasted until Schreiber's passing in 2004 at the age of 59.

In 1981, Duffy began working at CME as a runner for Schreiber's business, something Duffy called "the lowest form of humanity here at CME." In between trips from customer to broker with orders, Duffy observed the business and became fascinated by its energy and character.

"I remember the first day I walked into the old exchange over on Jackson Boulevard," said Duffy. "I could just remember the excitement, the roar, and trying to take it all in and trying to figure out what they were doing here."

A CME membership, however, seemed a distant possibility for an eager-to-trade Duffy. He first investigated leasing a membership, a much less expensive proposition, yet one that still carried a hefty price tag. Duffy, then 22 years old, determined that $50,000 could get him in the business of commodities trading with a leased seat. He discussed his plans with his parents. Duffy said:

My mother convinced my father to mortgage their [southwest-side Chicago] home. Now I had another brother and two sisters. So, unbeknownst to them, their next day might be out on the streets because we didn't have any reserves. That was it—a little city bungalow.

It actually put a lot of pressure on me as a young man to make sure that I didn't lose my family's home. ... I remember my mother convinced my father to do this, and then the bankers said to my father, "You've got to be out of your mind. He's 22 years old. You're going to let him go down and trade commodities at the Mercantile Exchange, and your future is your home? You've got to be crazy." My father said to the bankers and my mother, "It's our house. We believe in our son. We're going to let him. We're going to put this risk on him."

And so Duffy entered CME's legendary agricultural pits with some of the nation's most aggressive, spirited, and intelligent traders. Increasingly, he gained a sense of the business and the movements of the markets.

"Not that I understood what the hell a hog was or cattle was or a pork belly was, because I was born and raised in the city. I'd never been out of the city for the most part," Duffy said. "I never even went to the state fair. So I didn't know what a hog was, but I knew they went up and down."

For one year, Duffy continued leasing the membership and studying the market action.

By 1982, Duffy turned his attention to purchasing a CME seat.

"I didn't want to pay somebody forever," said Duffy. "Now that I'd been [somewhat] established, I got to know other traders who had been somewhat successful, and one particular trader came up to me and said, 'Terry, you've got to buy this seat.' I said to him I didn't have enough money. It's a $170,000 offer; it's a $150,000 bid. He said, 'I'll be your bank.'"

That arrangement spurred Duffy to buy a CME seat, one sold by meat giant Oscar Mayer & Company for $170,000. Before he could make his first payment, however, Duffy received a call from the man who had loaned him the $170,000 to purchase the CME seat. The trader had experienced a downturn in his fortunes and needed the money back quickly. The two trekked over to Harris Bank, where the trader's good relationships allowed him to transfer Duffy's debt to the bank. So Duffy incurred a $170,000 loan at 21 percent interest with no leeway.

"I'm really squeezed now. More than ever," Duffy recalled thinking.

But Duffy, raised on the city's south side and the product of working-class parents, invited good fortune with good doses of diligence and precision. In addition to his trading on the CME floor, he tended bar in the evenings at Shenanigans, a popular nightspot on the city's famed Rush Street corridor. He said:

> I was just doing whatever I could to make ends meet, and about two years into that mess ... business started to get really good. I started to develop more and more business on the floor, and I started to be able to pay off debt. My first priority was paying off my family's home for the money they originally loaned me.
>
> I learned one thing very, very early on in my career—and it was discipline. I was raised with good discipline. I was a natural, I think, for the speculative side of trading derivative products. You had to have discipline, and that's something I knew when I was 22 years old as a member here. I just knew when to cut my losses, and I was very fortunate.[1]

In the coming years, Duffy would ascend through CME's ranks and earn the respect of many peers. Stints as a pit chairman resulted in other traders encouraging him to run for CME's Board of Directors. Although defeated in his first attempt in 1992, Duffy returned to the ballot in 1995 and earned a seat on the Board. In April 2002, he rose to the position of Board chairman, overseeing CME's entry into the 21st century and the courageous moves to come.

Future CME Chairman Terry Duffy joined CME in 1981 as a runner. He rose to prominence in the exchange, earned a seat on the CME Board of Directors in 1995, and was elected chairman in 2002, setting the course for some of CME's boldest initiatives.

BRODSKY JOINS CME

JUST ONE MONTH AFTER WILLIAM J. BROD-sky's arrival at Chicago Mercantile Exchange in September 1982, the *Chicago Tribune* reported, "It's a sign of the times that William J. Brodsky doesn't know beans about pork bellies."[1]

Admittedly, Brodsky knew little about CME in the early 1980s, and he knew even less about the likes of pork bellies and cattle. What Brodsky did know, however, were stocks and options, a fitting avenue for him to enter the fray at CME, an institution fresh off its formation of the Index and Options Market (IOM) and investigating options on stock index futures and innovating the next wave of the futures industry.

In March 1982, conversations began among CME leaders looking to find a replacement for departing Executive Vice President Beverly

Splane. From a diverse set of candidates, Brodsky emerged the primary target. The 38-year-old Brodsky, an executive vice president at the New York–based American Stock Exchange (AMEX), intrigued CME for his pivotal role leading the options business at AMEX.[2] And, like many of CME's leaders, including Leo Melamed and Clayton K. Yeutter, Brodsky held a law degree, further endearing him to the CME hierarchy.

Brodsky boasted a long career on Wall Street. His father, Irwin, was a 61-year veteran of the securities industry and passed the interest on to his son. At 17, William Brodsky landed his first job on Wall Street as a floor runner at the NYSE. By the time Brodsky graduated from the head of his law class at Syracuse

From our side of the equation, we saw an opportunity to allow trading to go on more than eight or 10 hours a day. We contributed our expertise, and the government of Singapore contributed personnel and all the costs of setting up. Singapore got a thriving futures market, and we got the opportunity for our traders to offset during the night hours.[31]

On September 7, 1984, SIMEX opened, signaling the official start of the historic relationship between Chicago Mercantile Exchange and the Singapore-based exchange. The move proved to be both a simultaneous defensive and offensive move for CME. While it protected the Eurodollar contract from LIFFE's imposing hand, as well as other would-be suitors, the relationship also served to jump-start the move toward international relationships to secure new markets.[32]

"From the moment SIMEX opened its doors, we could actually watch the open interest in Eurodollars at LIFFE begin to falter. A few years later, its officials gave up the fight and delisted the contract," Melamed said. "The Merc–SIMEX connection made Singapore the financial futures beacon of Southeast Asia and allowed the IMM's Eurodollar

The triumvirate of (from left) Jack Sandner, Leo Melamed, and Clayton K. Yeutter would oversee CME's transition from the late 1970s into the mid-1980s, an era that witnessed the launch of the Eurodollar contract and the S&P 500 futures contract, bold ideas that would send CME into new financial arenas.

University, he accepted a post with Model, Roland & Company, continuing his relationship with the action of Wall Street. In 1974, Brodsky joined AMEX, eventually overseeing the stock options, market operations, trading analysis, and planning.[3]

In 1982, on the heels of the IOM creation and launch of the S&P 500 futures, CME recruited Brodsky, a lifelong New Yorker, to join the team at Chicago's upstart exchange. After three years as executive vice president, a tenure that witnessed Brodsky's reorganization of CME's administrative staff into a more efficient unit,[4] he assumed the role of president in 1985, replacing Yeutter.[5]

For the next dozen years, Brodsky guided CME through many of its most notable and tumultuous times. Brodsky's tenure as president witnessed the opening of the exchange's Tokyo office, launch of the original CME Globex system, expansion of the upper trading floor,

and release of CME's fastest-growing product, the E-mini S&P 500 futures contract. And he was, as CME leaders predicted upon his hire, an instrumental force in the exchange's development of stock index derivatives.

CME, however, endured one of the most chaotic days in its history with the stock market crash of 1987, an event that witnessed the Dow plunge more than 22 percent on Monday, October 19. That week, Brodsky's office became the war-room setting for CME's response to one of the nation's bleakest financial times on record. "The crash really was a week of horror rather than just a day," Brodsky recalled.[6]

In 1997, Brodsky, to the surprise of many, left CME to join another Chicago exchange, the Chicago Board Options Exchange (CBOE), as its CEO and chairman. There, in 2002, Brodsky led the CBOE's partnership with CME in the launch of OneChicago, a joint venture in the trading of single stock futures.

In 1984, CME established the first international link between a U.S. futures exchange and an overseas counterpart when it partnered with SIMEX. The partnership represented not only a merger of business but one of cultures as well, as many American traders ventured to Singapore to join their Asian colleagues on the SIMEX floor.

contract to become the greatest futures contract in history."[33]

Once again, CME had come to battle with a challenge, and, as it had more often than not in its history, the exchange had succeeded. The once-sleepy exchange—the house that pork bellies built—would continue its growth and, as always, reject complacency in favor of relentless innovation.

1987—CME membership approves move to create Globex, a global electronic trading platform, in October 6 referendum

1992—Globex, CME's after-hours electronic trading platform, begins operation

1997—CME introduces a smaller version of the S&P 500, the E-mini S&P 500 futures contract, which becomes the fastest-growing product ever launched by CME

1987—"Black Monday"—October 19 stock market suffers largest one-day decline in history, and the CME comes under fire

1993—CME opens its upper trading floor and becomes the world's largest physical marketplace with nearly two acres of trading space

1998—CME introduces the next generation of Globex II, the next comprehensive step in electronic trading

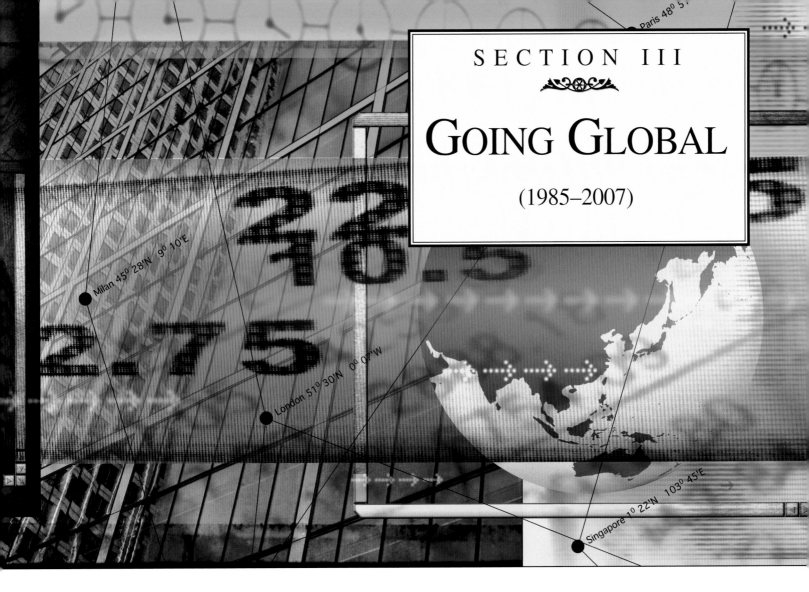

SECTION III

GOING GLOBAL

(1985–2007)

Paris 48° 5'

Milan 45° 28'N 9° 10'E

London 51° 30'N 0° 07'W

Singapore 1° 22'N 103° 45'E

2000—CME becomes the first U.S. financial exchange to demutualize by converting its membership interests into shares of common stock, trading separately from exchange trading privileges

2002—CME joins with Chicago Board Options Exchange and Chicago Board of Trade (CBOT) to launch OneChicago for trading of single-stock futures

2002—CME is listed on New York Stock Exchange, becoming the first financial futures exchange to be publicly traded

2003—CME and CBOT enter a common clearing agreement

2004—One billionth Globex transaction recorded

2004 to 2005—Eurodollar referendum passes, creating the dramatic shift of the Eurodollar contract from the trading floor to the Globex platform

2007— CME and CBOT merge to form CME Group

2006— CME is the world's largest and most diverse financial exchange handling more than one billion contracts each year valued more than $600 trillion

In August 1988, less than one year after the U.S. stock market crash, CME marked the milestone of 500,000 open interest in Eurodollars with a champagne celebration.

CHAPTER SEVEN

DEFENDER OF THE FREE MARKET

1985–1991

Our successes have come not only because we move rapidly, but also because we in the futures industry and all of us here at CME represent the true idea of voluntary, cooperative, free enterprise.

—Jack Sandner

THE DECADE OF PROSPERITY had settled upon both Chicago Mercantile Exchange (CME) and the rest of the nation. The bull market charged ahead in the United States, earning distinction as one of the nation's strongest ever. As the world trade and international investment markets experienced dramatic increases, the global financial arena became wealthier, more complex, and even more volatile.

Nowhere did the upswing in business and competitive financial maneuvering emerge more apparent than in Chicago. CME, in fact, broke its own trading records almost monthly, with the Standard & Poor's pits and a variety of options offerings leading the way.[1]

In April 1986, for instance, the exchange traded more than 6 million contracts, 1.8 million of which were contracts in stock index futures alone.[2] On May 21, nearly 80,000 currency options contracts traded hands, at the time the most currency options traded at an exchange on a single day. Membership prices in the Index and Options Market (IOM) division, which many CME and International Monetary Market (IMM) members had purchased for $30,000 in 1982, soared to $98,000.[3] The year 1986 ended with a record 68 million contracts traded on the CME floor, a record for the 10th consecutive year, prompting CME Chairman Jack Sandner to claim, "We are a valuable commodity in ourselves."[4]

In the United States, President Ronald Reagan, espousing a free-market philosophy, maintained the idea that free enterprise and the competition it sparks would make the most of the nation's—and the world's—vast economic resources. Few subscribed to that idea more passionately than leaders of CME. Not only was a free-market attitude the right approach, it was the only approach, an enthusiasm evident in the exchange's long-held "free markets for free men" mantra—the same mantra that Sandner wore embroidered on his trading jacket. The bull market overtaking the nation's financial arena symbolized the ideals of both capitalism and democracy working in disciplined harmony.

With the ongoing globalization of financial markets, CME continued its pursuit of overseas markets and participants. The exchange's 1984 deal with the Singapore International Monetary Exchange (SIMEX) highlighted CME's commitment to the formation of a global exchange. On September 3, 1986, CME

CME Chairman Jack Sandner (left) joined former CME chairman and longtime trader Bill Katz on September 18, 1991, to celebrate the 30th anniversary of the pork belly contract—a contract that all but saved the exchange from extinction in the early 1960s.

opened its Nikkei 225 futures contract at SIMEX. The contract, based on Japan's most observed stock average, the Nikkei Stock Average, and the world's second largest stock market, neatly mimicked the S&P 500 contract.[5] In addition, the contract illustrated the markets' adaptability over time zones, oceans, and cultures.

In his 1987 chairman's letter, Sandner praised the CME culture and its members:

We are not the kind to rest on our laurels. The Chicago Mercantile Exchange is restless, dynamic, ever on the move. Our exchange is imbued with the spirit of its members.[6]

Celebrating SIMEX's opening of its Nikkei 225 contract were (from left): Akinobu Kojima, president and CEO of QUICK Corporation; Ang Swee Tian, general manager of SIMEX; Ko Morita, president and CEO of NKS; Ng Kok Song, chairman of the Monetary Authority of Singapore; Leo Melamed, special counsel of CME; and Jack Sandner, CME chairman.

Signs of Trouble

In 1986, the nation's strongest bull market refused to slow. Increasingly, however, CME leaders considered what impact a negative market turn might have on the futures industry. Many exchange leaders voiced concern that the bull market's charge was slowing; many more understood that CME's S&P pit would be among the first to share any depressing financial news.

"What worried me," said Melamed, "was that on the day of reckoning, our S&P contract would be the first to signal the bad news to the world. And I knew what people did to messengers with bad news."[7]

Other problems outside of an anticipated market decline had also begun to surface. In the S&P pit, for instance, hundreds of traders stood elbow to elbow in a space no bigger than a tennis court. While congestion remained a major problem, so, too, did volatility and questions of efficient trading mechanisms or quotations. Price quotations would sometimes lag 50 points behind real-time prices.[8]

Above: In January 1987, the nation's bull market was charging ahead on the CME trading floor, where action in the pits was furious and filled with bodies. Ten months later, however, the floor would tell a different story as the strongest-ever bull market would come to a crashing halt.

Left: Traders began their newest venture at the exchange on June 16, 1987, as trading in gold futures opened.

In August 1986, exchange leaders responded to these issues by forming a committee headed by IOM Governor Howard Dubnow and CME members Harry Lowrance and Robert Hammer to study the S&P pits and determine effective solutions.[9] Exchange leaders openly wondered if CME, for all of its progress, shuffled along using outdated methods, namely open outcry. Moreover, dual trading increasingly surfaced as a hot-button issue, one that would serve to cause immense conflict among CME leaders, members, and traders.

Meanwhile, on January 8, 1987, the Dow Jones Industrial Average topped the 2,000 mark for the first time in history. The success of the nation's economy was met with much adulation and celebration; many, however, cheered with some reservations, wondering how much longer the history's strongest bull market could last.[10] The previous year had concluded with a CME trading record of 216 million contracts, as financial futures gained prominence as highly valued, global risk-management tools.[11]

While relishing CME's growing profile in the financial industry, CME leaders considered plans to insulate the market from any actual market downturn. In an uncharacteristic move, the exchange pursued efforts to establish price limits on the S&P contract. Jack Sandner appointed a committee to study the issue. However, the idea met with resistance from the Futures Industry Association and members.

Inside Action

Melamed and Sandner sent a letter to S&P 500 traders, charging that the exchange leadership was determined to handle trader violations with swift and harsh consequences. Within a week, CME's self-regulatory and reform-minded efforts took hold with numerous fines, as well as the expulsion of two traders. In addition, surveillance procedures and internal review initiatives were also introduced.[12]

Through a proposal, CME then moved to restrict dual trading. Dual trading involved a broker filling customer orders while trading for himself, thus creating a potential conflict of interest. The Board also drafted a proposal placing limits on trading within a broker group, which made CME the first such exchange to attempt the restriction of broker group trading.[13] The proposal addressed the problem of having a group of traders changing contracts among themselves, rather than exposing the contract to the entire pit.

Approval from the Commodity Futures Trading Commission (CFTC) was granted on May 15, 1987, signifying a major self-regulatory accomplishment for the exchange. CME leaders knew well that dedication to maintaining fair and efficient trading practices was paramount for the continued growth of the markets.

A Global Exchange

On May 22, 1987, CME opened an office in Tokyo, yet another signal of the exchange's mounting global presence. With offices in London and Singapore already established, the move to Tokyo landed CME in another key market. Yet CME, with ambitions to grow the world's first global exchange, increasingly saw that technology had the ability to traverse water and land to connect market-users throughout the world. This drove CME to initiate plans to create a global electronic marketplace, one that would truly allow the exchange to become the world's preeminent market center with an after-hours trading platform.

"[The Ministry of Finance was] so pleased that we opened the office that [he] announced on the day of our opening that Japanese institutions could use U.S. futures markets," said CME President William

J. Brodsky, who was elected to the exchange's top post in 1985 with the departure of Clayton K. Yeutter. "And it was very important because the Eurodollar was just becoming an important international product and there was a potential market."[14]

Beginning in 1986, CME's Strategic Planning Committee, chaired by Melamed, conducted a year-long comprehensive study of the critical issues facing the futures industry. The committee isolated three specific issues—globalization, automation, and off-exchange expansion—and argued that an "after-hours" transaction system represented a single response to all three concerns.[15] CME's relationship with SIMEX, one that allowed members access to the other markets during off-trading hours, proved the value and inherent potential of markets in separate time zones. Yet that alone, reasoned the committee, would not be sufficient. The futures industry needed to take bold new steps, and CME would lead the way.

"Financial managers no longer wait for local markets to open before responding," Melamed, said. "Rather, they have the capacity to initiate immediate market positions, a capacity that has come to be known as globalization. With globalization, each financial center has become a direct competitor to all others, offering new opportunities, challenges, and perils."[16]

In an article appearing in a special edition of the venerable financial magazine *Barron's*, Melamed wrote of the exchange's plans, "The Chicago Mercantile Exchange's response to the demands of globalization combines elements of electronic linkage with those of extended trading and integrates them with the open-outcry system. In effect, it attempts to draw the best from the past and present and marry it to the technology of the future."[17]

On March 24, 1987, CME's Strategic Planning Committee charged Ken Cone with contacting Reuters Holdings PLC and Telerate to discuss the possibilities of an after-hours electronic trading system.[18] For its shared goals and global credibility, Reuters emerged the logical choice to join CME in its venture to create an electronic market platform. Over the next several months, CME leaders met with Reuters officials to negotiate a deal. On September 2, the parties announced a joint venture to create a global electronic trading system

In April 1987, CME leaders traveled to Japan to celebrate the opening of CME's Tokyo office. The exchange's arrival in Japan afforded CME the opportunity to gain more market participants.

called Post Market Trade (PMT).[19] The agreement, an exclusive deal between CME and Reuters covering 12 years, was heralded by Sandner as "a revolutionary milestone in the development of futures trade."[20]

Immediately, the exchange felt the positive impact of the announcement, as membership seats in CME, IMM, and IOM all set record prices on September 3, 1987.[21] Though excitement and energy were high, CME still needed its members to throw their support behind the deal in a referendum scheduled for October.

In the days leading up to the vote, exchange leaders prepared an educational campaign aimed at members. More than 1,000 members attended an informational meeting a week prior to the refer-

endum, many expressing concern regarding what an electronic exchange would mean for them. For some traders, particularly the local independents who relied upon the sacred ground of the pits, PMT signaled the end of their careers. Others, however, recognized the potential benefit of such a program.

Terry Duffy, a young agricultural trader who had made good in the trading pit and later became CME chairman, explained:

I think that originally some members felt that was the end of their business; others felt this could be a windfall for them because originally Globex was set up for the benefit of the members. Through the PMT partnership, they would derive all the benefits from electronic trading. So they saw that as an ongoing dividend stream. So it was kind of a two-fold approach. The younger guys looked at it as the end of their livelihood; the older guys looked at it as, "I'm not going to trade anymore, and I'm going to get a dividend forever."

I will say, at first blush, I thought that was the end of business as we knew it. We knew a little bit about electronics ... but we didn't know how or what it could do to our business. When it was introduced here in 1987, here at CME, I think a lot of us thought it was the end of an era, even though it was just the beginning of a new one.[22]

Much of the concern resided in the unknown territories that stood before the exchange and its members, both the electronic system's impact on their careers and the practical application of technology.

"There was a lot of trepidation over the [PMT] system naturally," said Craig Donohue, who joined CME in 1989, when the exchange was preparing for the launch of its electronic system. "A lot of people were making a very good living trading and filling orders on the floor, and I think the trepidation was not only, 'Will it change our livelihoods?' But I think

there also was the fear of technology, 'Just how will we adapt? Will we use it? Will we be able to use it?'"[23]

Despite the concerns, the PMT referendum passed unanimously on October 6, 1987, and CME Globex, the new name for the PMT program—suggested by Sandner—transitioned from idea into reality.[24]

"The membership trusted the Board and what they said," said David Gomach, whose work with CME began in March 1987 as a manager for budgeting and financial analysis. "But there were a couple of years of process on just how we were going to structure it and how we were going to sell it to membership, while at the same time, we really had to change the culture of the organization."[25]

But with CME Globex, CME was once again anticipating the future and seeking to advance the institution's innovative culture. "Think about CME Globex as an innovation that the exchange put in place. It took a lot of pain. It was a big threat," said Nobel Prize–winning economist Myron Scholes. "The technology was not perfect at the time, but the idea of seeing that electronic trading was going to be the wave of the future even though launching that in '87 and bearing the cost and the patience to bring CME Globex to fruition was a brilliant idea."[26]

The Anatomy of a Crash

The nation's bull market had held an unrelenting grip on the American economy throughout much of the 1980s. It was a grip, however, beginning to weaken, despite all the outward signs of positive financial energy. Falling interest rates, a weak U.S. dollar, and budget deficits signaled the danger ahead. The months of Dow-watching culminated in August 1987, when the Dow Jones Industrial Average peaked at 2,722.[27] From that peak, a slow decline began.

"There were a number of things going on in the overall economy," said the then-CME

Leo Melamed (left) and Jack Sandner (center) joined Reuters executive Andre Villeneuve (right) in announcing the partnership to form an electronic postmarket trading venue. Later termed CME Globex, a merger of the words "global" and "exchange," traders at CME responded with conflicting opinions.

head of the Clearinghouse John Davidson. "Basically, all the way through August and September, there was a very strong rally in the stock market and, at the same time, the Fed had been consistently raising interest rates. For whatever reason ... the market came to the conclusion ... that the increase in interest rates was eventually going to close off the growth in the economy in such a way that corporate earnings couldn't be sustained at the level they had been while prices were running up. People decided it was time to adjust their equity portfolios."[28]

In the week of October 12 to 16, 1987, the impending doom that would soon befall the market began shifting into overdrive. On Wednesday, October 14, the Dow remained above 2,500. By Friday, the Dow had fallen 250 points, a 10 percent decline, and created a flurry of sell orders.[29]

"The interesting thing was, virtually everybody in a senior position in the industry, the futures industry, was at the FIA expo," said Davidson of Friday, October 16. "There were a series of panels, and people's beepers kept going off in the middle of these panels ... and people would come back into the session with a somewhat worried look on their faces. Then the beeper would go off again."[30]

CME leaped into action. In an unprecedented move, the exchange called for an out-trade session over the weekend to clear up discrepancies between trades that had occurred from Friday's furious open-outcry session. Though the flood of Friday's sell orders were settled, the exchange's nerves remained tense. On Sunday afternoon, exchange leaders began monitoring the Asian markets, including the Nikkei 225, and the opening of their Monday trade session. As sell orders in Asia and Europe accumulated, confusion and panic consumed the world's economy. In Tokyo, Hong Kong, Sydney, London, Paris, Madrid, Zurich, and nearly every overseas financial center, the merciless grip of Black Monday had taken hold—and had done so while America's traders were sleeping during the transition of Sunday to Monday.

"We knew there was this tremendous amount of volatility in the market ... [and] it was clear that a downdraft was going to continue from that. As the European markets opened in the early hours of the morning, they also were declining precipitously. So we knew that ours were going to follow," Davidson said.[31]

The only question remaining in exchange leaders' minds was just how hard the market would fall. The day CME leaders had long dreaded arrived with a deafening bang, one heard reverberating around the world.

"The unfortunate thing about the crash is that we knew it was coming. That Friday afternoon before the crash, the markets were in terrible shape," said CME President Bill Brodsky. "The crash was really a week of horror rather than just a day."[32]

Black Monday—October 19, 1987

October 19, 1987, is called Black Monday for a reason. It stands among the darkest days in the nation's financial history, a day that witnessed the charging bull market run headfirst into a wall of despair.

"There's a very subtle difference, a very thin line, from when you go from a sell-off into a panic mode, and that's what happened," said CME member Barry Lind. "We never like to see panic."[33]

Sandner arrived at CME at 4:00 A.M. and joined Brodsky in his office. At that point, they began to coordinate an open communication channel with the regulatory agencies, banks, and clearing firms.

By 7:00 A.M., Melamed had established what would be a long-running dialogue with the New York Stock Exchange (NYSE) and its chairman, John J. Phelan, Jr., as well as other U.S. exchanges and the government. All parties were aware of the daunting road ahead. An hour before opening at the NYSE, Phelan told Melamed that sell orders were piling up in unprecedented numbers.

Sandner, whose firm was home for a number of S&P traders, put on his trading jacket, went down to the trading pit for the opening and stayed for the first hour. He said:

It was a debacle. Traders were trying to make a market, but the market fall was unrelenting. It didn't stop to take a breath. The trader's bids were being swallowed whole as the market searched and probed for the next bid. It was a force that kept multiplying, a force that no trader had ever faced.[34]

The S&P 500 market opened at 8:30 A.M. at 261.50, a drop of nearly 21 points from Friday's

Headlines in the Wake of the Crash

Day to Remember in Financial District
—New York Times

Washington Quiet as Wall St. Panics
—New York Times

The Crash of '87:
The Market Debacle Rouses Worst Fears of Little Investors—
Many Are Beginning to Talk in Terms of Doomsday;
Big Investors Are Braver
—Wall Street Journal

Upheaval in the Financial World:
Hopes Sink as Stocks Slip
—New York Times

Wall St. Panic Historic Drop—
Dow Falls 508 Points
—Chicago Sun Times

Bears Maul Market:
508-point Loss Wipes Out Years Gain
—Chicago Tribune

close.[35] Almost immediately, alarm and fear struck the trading floor—emotions that would command the day. By 1:15 P.M., CME's S&P 500 contract had fallen by more than 5,000 points, a sign of the day's bleak reality and one that CME relayed to the nation.

"It was just an unbelievable time. Basically, the whole floor stopped and was just focusing on the S&P 500 pit, and you just couldn't believe the velocity of the downward trend of all the prices," said Marty Gepsman, a one-time IOM Board member and floor trader. "It was just like we've never seen anything like this. You know, just with our mouths open. Oh, my God, and oohing and aahing after another 10 points or whatever was ticked down in the S&P 500. It was just unbelievable."[36]

By day's end, the Dow had fallen an astonishing 508 points, a 22.6 percent drop, which was nearly double the previous record plunge of 12.8 percent experienced in October 1929 that signaled the beginning of the Great Depression.[37] Black Monday had ended in a roar of disappointment, leaving financial ruin in its wake. Trader Randy McKay said:

The market was falling, and it seemed to accelerate as it fell. It would fall five points in 10 minutes, and then it would fall 10 points in the next 10 minutes, and it would fall 20 points in the following

period of time. And it just accelerated and accelerated all day. It looked early on that it was a normal down day—no big deal—but then it just kept going faster and faster, until the last half-hour or 45 minutes, it must have fallen half of that 500 points.[38]

Traders on Wacker Drive, meanwhile, maintained a sense of disbelief, coupled with emotions running high. It was a monumental day in the nation's history—if not the world's—and CME traders were shocked at its sheer force.

"There was certainly confusion. There was certainly a lot of panicking. But mostly it was kind of incredulity," said McKay. "Five-hundred points on the Dow was unheard of, and nobody could believe that it could go any further, but it kept going and going."[39]

At CME, S&P 500 traders felt the impact of the day's wrath—both financially and in a growing public relations battle that would find many fingers pointed at them. The S&P 500 index plunged 80.75 points on Black Monday, a 28.6 percent decline.[40]

"On Monday, the brunt of the downdraft in the market was taken from our perspective by the people in the S&P 500 futures and related options pits," said Davidson. "There was some impact in the interest rate pits, but Monday was really all about stock index futures."[41]

When the market closed, CME's clearing and settlement division prepared for a long and tense night. Because CME employs a no-debt, pay-as-you-go system, all pays and collects in futures had to be settled in cash prior to the next day's opening, unlike the securities industry in which trades had five days to clear.

A settlement sum of $2.53 billion resided in the clearinghouse, a radical departure from the $120 million CME would witness on an average trading day.[42] As such, CME needed to clear trades and collect in order to open on Tuesday, an impera-

Trader Ben Rubin reacts to the day's bleak happenings on October 19, 1987. Black Monday, as it was called, would prove to be the largest one-day decline in the nation's financial history, causing panic, fear, and concern to pulsate through exchanges across the nation, including CME.

tive move that would serve as a sign of normalcy amid the chaos. The settlement banks and the CME clearinghouse worked all night to settle the accounts.

The Critical Call

At 5:30 A.M., Davidson informed Sandner that there was a big problem because a large investment bank did not settle a $660 million pay. After determining that the monies were available in the firm's bank, but were being held as a result of the chaos, Sandner made a critical call. He telephoned the chairman of the investment bank and laid out the situation; Sandner quickly realized that the investment official was unfamiliar with the no-debt system used in futures. The official did not appreciate the urgency to wire the money before the markets opened. Then Sandner spoke the words to move the investment chairman to action:

I must be candid. If you don't push the button, the headline will read "Morgan Stanley Defaults." The CME will not open, and the panic that ensues will make Monday's crash look like a warm up.[43]

Morgan Stanley's Chairman S. Parker Gilbert pushed the button.

The Days That Followed

Just before 7:20 A.M. on Tuesday, the storm that had hammered the exchange and its clearinghouse subsided, and CME opened its doors, thereby avoiding a deluge of added financial chaos across the nation.[44]

On Tuesday, the market swung up and down like a pendulum, rallying only to then falter. At exchanges across the country, including the Chicago Board Options Exchange and the American Stock Exchange, the doors closed.

That left the NYSE and CME as the nation's sole markets with any power to alter the flow of the tide that day. Securities and Exchange Commission (SEC) Chairman David Ruder then told reporters that the SEC might consider a brief trading halt.[42] Late Tuesday morning, NYSE Chairman Phelan told CME leaders the New York exchange was meeting to decide whether to close its markets, thereby leaving CME in a precarious position.[43]

Melamed and Sandner initiated efforts to protect the exchange, including instituting a temporary halt to trading. In telling floor traders of the temporary stoppage, Melamed made his point, "We cannot be left alone for everyone to dump on us."[45]

Within 15 minutes, however, CME leaders learned the NYSE would not close, and immediately trading in the CME pits resumed. A corporate buy-back program had allowed recovery to seep into the marketplace. Slowly, the market rebounded—a process that would cover many days and generate a swell of emotions.

"On Wednesday," Davidson said, "we got back to a somewhat more normal level of volume and volatility, and it was clear that things were going to work out."[46]

By week's end, the nation's financial legs steadied. While some traders exited the bedlam of the pits with its life-changing swings in one direction or the other, many more walked away from the CME building on Friday weary, yet safe and determined. For nearly every trader, however, the crash of 1987 symbolized the uncompromising power of the markets, the unbiased movements that take no prisoners. Veteran trader Yra Harris observed:

[The market] is the most objective force in our lives. [It doesn't care] who you are. It doesn't care if your last name is Kennedy or whatever. It doesn't care. It makes no difference.[47]

The Bull's Eye Exchange

"The whole world was looking for somebody to blame, so I would say that was the truly dangerous fallout from the stock market crash, the fight to preserve the integrity of the futures markets against attacks from people who were just looking for scapegoats," said CME outside counsel Jerry Salzman.[48]

In the immediate wake of the 1987 crash, CME earned unwanted attention in the form of criticism and charges of instigating the crash. As Jack Sandner once said, "Everyone seems to know the headlines but not the story."[49]

"When the market crashed," said David Gomach, budgeting and finance manager, "every effort that the exchange had [went] into defending its position of how the exchange didn't exacerbate the crash but actually helped prevent it from being worse. Still, there were a lot of questions and doubt as to whether we were going to be a scapegoat and what 1988 was going to be like and the years afterward."[50]

In December 1987, the NYSE sponsored a report that questioned the function of futures markets, throwing a forceful punch at the automation of stock index futures and options.[51] CME defended itself, contending that the NYSE floor was unequipped to deal with the massive sell of orders that hammered the nation's economy on October 19.[52] Sandner said:

The Chicago Mercantile Exchange was providing liquidity to the market that nobody else could provide. When the market turned, it turned here because we kept the market going. We kept liquidity in the market. So we shouldn't be branded with this horrible letter on our chest. We should be celebrated.[53]

Additional commentaries on the crash named program trading, portfolio insurance, and arbitrage as culprits, thus sending Chicago's problems to the floor of the NYSE. A trio of CFTC reports, the first in 1987 and a pair of follow-ups in 1988, however, found that index arbitrage and portfolio insurance served only a small role in the day's events and exonerated CME from culpability in the stock market crash.[54] Perhaps the major factor that characterized the day was the fact that the decline occurred in one day rather than being spread over days or weeks.

"The breakdown was not because of a 500-plus-point change in value in the securities market," Sandner testified before members of Congress in April 1988. "Rather, the system was threatened because the change happened in one day. The speed of the change caused the banking and credit system, the securities exchanges, and the futures and options exchanges to be stretched to their limits."[55]

Despite the facts, however, CME and the futures market found criticism wherever it turned; all CME leaders could do was address questions directly with the facts. The futures industry, they said, did its intended job during the crash. It transferred risk in a liquid market. The industry gained a credible ally in Princeton University economist Burton G. Malkiel, who wrote in a *New York Times* editorial:

The futures markets arose to cope with this increased underlying volatility. Thus blaming futures and program trading for the volatility is as illogical as blaming the thermometer for measuring uncomfortable temperatures.[56]

Lessons Learned

Amid the fallout and critical charges, CME's Board of Directors moved aggressively to approve measures that would aid in assuring the safety and soundness of the clearinghouse. Within two years, CME established a program with the Options Clearing Corporation to help eliminate faltering cash flows and to allow for cross-margining, a procedure for margining related securities, options, and futures contracts jointly, when different clearing organizations clear each side of the position.[57]

"There's cross-margining now between the options exchanges and [the futures markets]. It was the first time it was put into play between the securities exchanges and the futures exchanges," said Rick Redding, who joined CME's research department in 1988, while safeguarding discussions intensified. "One of the important things after 1987 was we then began trading position information every day amongst the exchanges ... so we could get a look at overall risk."[58]

In the aftermath of the crash, price limits between the securities and the futures exchanges also became a reality, instituted by the CFTC and SEC. Combined with the voluntary efforts of both CME and the NYSE to institute a series of "circuit breakers" and "shock absorbers" to protect against another drastic fall, the nation's exchanges demonstrated their unwavering determination to prevent another Black Monday.

The 1987 crash also taught the expanding financial world some important lessons, ones felt in the boardrooms as well as on the trading floors. Fear paralyzed much of the day, while respect for the markets served as a valuable antidote. Davidson said:

There's a lot of lessons to be learned from [the crash]. First of all, we learned lessons about the magnitude of price moves and lessons about the need for orderly markets. And, while you don't want to have price limits that artificially constrain the price level from getting to the right place, if you have some speed bumps along the way, it actually gives people a chance to think about [the facts at hand]. "Am I just responding to the big net change number I see on the screen, or do I understand the fundamentals?" The interconnections between the stock market and the futures market and the options market hadn't been as appreciated as well as they were previously.[59]

Todd Petzel, who joined CME following the crash to head the exchange's financial research group, argued that diversification became a buzzword following the crash.

"The main message [regarding CME's strength after the crash] was that every strong financial institution needs multiple tools," he said. "Long-term investors who buy stocks and put them in a portfolio and hold them for years and years are perfectly well-served by the stock market, but there are a whole lot of people who actually add liquidity to the system and make it more efficient for those long-term investors to operate, who really don't need risk-management tools like options and futures. Without them, we've seen in every market around the world that they're less efficient, less liquid, and ultimately, of less use to the end users."[60]

For some traders on the CME floor, however, the ultimate result of the crash proved to be a change in attitude, a change in perspective, and a stark appreciation for the market's unwavering knowledge. Duffy recalled a shift in the trading culture in the weeks following the crash:

All eyes were focused on the equity side of the trading floor. So whether you were trading agricultural products or not, your eyes were focused on the equities. What happened was, there was so much money lost in the equities, it was affecting positions in other markets. So whether you were fundamentally right in the agricultural market, you could be economically wrong, because of the pressures to sell those products, because of the margin calls they had in the equity complex. So it affected all markets, [and] it was a different way of trading for quite some time after that.[61]

Turning the Corner

After the 1987 crash, the nation's bull market witnessed the end of its long run. In the latter years of the decade, and during the transition into the 1990s, CME turned its attention to technology. Once a topic that traders dreaded, the technological wave sweeping the nation encouraged exchange leaders to continue its path with CME Globex and other technological initiatives. Moreover, the closing of the decade provided CME and other financial entities with a chance to test the numerous post-crash reforms.

On Friday, October 13, 1989, the Dow Jones fell 190.58 points. The post-crash safeguards were activated, and trading at CME paused for 30 minutes, while the stock exchanges responded. The next business day, Monday, October 16, the market recovered with a remarkable 88.12 point upswing.[62] In the process, futures markets, which ran ahead of

---

For all its steps toward globalization, CME nevertheless remained an institution grounded in its city and seeking to invest in its future. In 1990, CME Chairman John T. Geldermann visited with a group of Chicago students after CME pledged to donate computers to the city's public schools.

securities in price reporting, were justified as a legitimate and valuable tool for users, a welcome shift from the condemnation heaved at the exchange and the futures industry after the 1987 crash.

In early 1990, CME released its agenda-setting "Blueprint for the 1990s," listing six objectives:

- *Resolve current trading rule issues and establish a transaction process "beyond reproach."*
- *Settle all differences that divide the membership.*
- *Resolve regulatory and margin issues relating to equity index futures and options.*
- *Employ the Globex strategy as the centerpiece of the exchange's international strategy.*
- *Seek new revenue sources for members by establishing the CME Resource and Service Company.*
- *Prepare the exchange to compete in spheres of trade from which it was then excluded.*[63]

In a letter to membership, CME Chairman Jack Sandner captured the character of the exchange and its goals when he said:

It is clear that CME is strategically positioned to forge the path toward globalization of the world's markets and to reap its rewards.[64]

The crash urged CME and other exchanges to pause and reflect, evaluating the present state of the nation's economy, as well as its future. With formidable modifications in places and the panic of the crash fading from traders' minds, CME turned all its attention ahead, just as it had done through-

On March 5, 1990, Leo Melamed announced he would take a step back from his leading role in matters at CME. Although he would continue to play an active role in the exchange's subsequent progress, Melamed's public announcement signaled the end of his nearly quarter-century run as CME's influential and spirited leader.

out its history. The 1990s, the exchange leaders determined, would be a decade of even greater progress and innovation, thereby setting the stage for CME's transition into the 21st century and its position as the world's elite futures marketplace.

By night, a worker cleans up the chaotic remains left behind by traders after a hectic day on the CME floor.

CHAPTER EIGHT

BUILDING FOR THE FUTURE

1991–1999

*CME is one of the few bright spots on a depressing economic landscape.
Our seats are trading at near-record prices, while membership values at
other exchanges are languishing. Our volume and open interest continue to
set records. Our markets continue to increase in efficiency and utility. Risk
and asset managers the world over look to us—for expertise, for proficiency.*

— Jack Sandner

SETTLING INTO THE FINAL decade of the 20th century, CME honored the spirit of its past, while pursuing its future with aggressive and insightful business initiatives.

In truth, such energy was nothing new. In the early 1970s, with the eventual collapse of the Bretton Woods Agreement looming and the need to trade in foreign currencies pressing on financial minds— CME leaders responded with the creation of the International Monetary Market (IMM), a move hailed as one of the most significant financial innovations of the century's final decades. In the 1980s, the exchange anticipated the lure of stock index futures contracts and responded with the Index and Options Market (IOM) and the S&P 500 Index futures, a firm recognition of risk management's increasing pace in the world economy.

In 1986, CME began internal discussions to pursue a pre- and post-market transaction system. CME leaders took the next step in CME's remarkable evolution by merging trade and technology. The exchange's 1987 agreement with Reuters to create a global electronic trading platform came to fruition in 1992, as the CME Globex system ushered in a new era of CME business, one that transcended national borders and time zones, the greatest obstacles to the financial world's globalization. Perhaps ironically, CME found an unlikely partner in the Chicago Board of Trade (CBOT), its

longtime rival and Chicago's granddaddy exchange. In 1990, the CBOT joined the CME Globex venture after abandoning its own plans for an electronic exchange. In 1991, Leo Melamed was elected as chairman of CME Globex Corporation.[1]

CME Globex, however, did not arrive without its own glitches. Technical problems, particularly the challenge of handling heavy volume days, consistently delayed CME Globex's release date. Similarly, awaiting new technology and computers also delayed the system's arrival. The revised CME Globex launch dates did little to earn the faith of the financial community, as many in the industry began questioning the system's credibility, forcing both CME and CBOT to devise new plans to lure sign-up partners. As of summer 1991, only French-based Marche a Terme International de France (MATIF) had joined the CME Globex show, while New York, London, and the Far East exchanges maintained their distance. Despite the setbacks, CME leaders remained steadfast in their desire to create a sound trading platform, regardless of public pressure, and they retained the

In 1991, Jack Sandner was elected to his seventh term as chairman of CME. Sandner ran and won the next three elections, finishing his long-term run as chairman in January 1998.

electronic trading would only gain momentum as days turned to years.

Although officially launched, its volume remained well below its potential for several reasons. First, the technology that would later catapult it to its subsequent prominence was still in development and years away from fruition. Second,

Left: On May 7, 1992, CME Chairman Jack Sandner (right) escorted former Soviet President Mikhail Gorbachev on a tour of the CME floor as traders clamored for handshakes. As the leader of the once-Communist stronghold, Gorbachev's visit to CME showed him the promises of the free enterprise system.

Below: CME Chairman Jack Sandner (left) poses with Globex Chairman Leo Melamed (center) and CME President William J. Brodsky (right) in 1992 to commemorate the Globex electronic trading system, one that would help advance the marriage of technology and futures trading. Globex began operation on June 25, 1992.

wish to launch the entire system at one time rather than in phases.

"I think we made a mistake by setting an overly ambitious schedule," Chairman Jack Sandner told the *Chicago Tribune.* "After all, we are creating the wheel for the first time. We are constantly refining the system's software and its hardware because when we do launch Globex, we want it to be free of all problems, and we want it to be user-friendly."[2]

The time to unveil CME Globex arrived on Thursday, June 25, 1992. After four years of planning and an investment of more than $75 million, four contracts were listed on CME Globex—Japanese yen, deutsche mark, yen-deutsche mark cross-rate futures, and the CBOT's 10-year Treasury note contract. By Friday morning at 6:00 A.M., the end of the overnight session, nearly 2,000 trades had occurred in the system's first 12 hours, from 200 terminals placed in Chicago, New York, London, and Paris.[3] The modest results matched the realistic expectations of CME and CBOT officials who were convinced that

CME Globex operated only in an after-hours mode. The eventual side-by-side operation, which simultaneously allowed instruments for trading both electronically and by open outcry, was not adopted until the end of the century.

The battle between those who favored open outcry and those who promoted electronic trade had been fomenting for years. The resulting strife precipitated major rifts among segments of the membership, created an array of political issues and adversities, and contributed to the decline in membership values. Ultimately, CME Globex protagonists prevailed, but not without a good deal of infighting and acrimony.

"I have said from the outset that Globex was not going to take off with a bang, but that it was going to grow slowly as market-users around the world would grow accustomed to the system," Sandner said just days after the system's release.[4]

The mere unveiling of CME Globex proved a success regardless of the numbers, an overwhelming sign that CME was committed to creating a global exchange in the present and future. "[Globex] had missed the right 'timing' window by a good two years. By now, every exchange in the world could boast some kind of electronic trade," said Melamed, who chaired the CME Globex committee. "Still, Globex was the only international trading system around, all the others were no more than glorified local area networks. Its future was made no less brighter by its delayed implementation."[5]

The CME Globex platform, the first global electronic trading system for futures and options, would become the world's premier market for derivative trading. With continuous enhancements, the platform would effectively enable CME to transform itself into a leading high-tech, global financial derivatives exchange.

Ten years later, with new contracts and the second generation of CME Globex implemented, the October 2002 average daily volume reached 1.2 million contracts. Throughout its history, CME Globex would achieve significant milestones as a result of successful electronic trading.

Chicago, That Financial Town

In 1992, CME continued riding on a wave of good fortune. In addition to the release of CME Globex, the exchange teamed with the CBOT, the Chicago Board Options Exchange, and, to a lesser degree, the Midwest Stock Exchange, to make Chicago the nation's new financial epicenter, particularly in the futures arena.

"Yet they remain," wrote *Chicago Tribune* journalist William B. Crawford, Jr., in a tome on the exchanges, "much like prophets in their own land—infrequently appreciated and sometimes viewed with deep cynicism by members of the non-investing public."[6]

For its part, neither CME nor its fellow Chicago exchanges were willing to cower. In addition to 150,000 jobs and $11 million in annual property taxes, the four exchanges provided the city with a strong amount of national respect.[7] Two decades earlier, with the opening of the IMM, New Yorkers had scoffed at the idea of Chicago's pork belly peddlers taking a shot at sophisticated trading. By the early 1990s, however, the city had dashed its way to the front of the nation's economy and soon shed the label that put the city's exchanges on par with Las Vegas' blackjack tables. With CME and CBOT, Chicago held nearly 50 percent of the market on futures and options on futures traded annually around the world.[8] No longer did Chicago play second fiddle; the same truth applied to CME, a sleepy exchange that awoke to find itself at the forefront of financial innovation and the world's risk-management needs. Sandner told the *Chicago Tribune*:

> *Our volume in 1991 was up around 6 percent, another record. The Eurodollar contract has reached open interest of more than a trillion dollars; we have broken many records in our currency contracts, all because the world has discovered risk management, and because we offer a broad spectrum of trading products that enables money managers across the globe to manage that risk.*
>
> *It is tremendously exciting to be involved in a critical industry at a critical time in the history of the world. In a way, the world has been stood on its head. Ten years ago, it was malfeasance for money managers to use our markets; today, it is malfeasance for them not to use them.*[9]

Chicago and its exchanges had risen to a position of paramount importance in the global economy, one extending its reach and greeting new participants each day. At CME, the exchange's ascent to heights of the world's financial markets served as a vindication of capitalism, the Chicago way, and above all, the tenacity and spirit of an exchange intent on proving the cynics wrong, the dreamers right.

For the fourth time in two decades, however, CME's tremendous growth found expense as a companion on the journey. Once again, CME needed to inflate its physical space. This time, the expansion would require neither pleas to the mayor nor a search for new real estate. In a move brilliant for its foresight, CME's building of 30 South Wacker Drive in the early 1980s included a vacant upper trading floor that could add up to 30,000 square feet of trading space. As the exchange continued to

blossom and traders consumed every inch of available floor space, the decision to open the upper trading floor was announced in 1992.

Less than a week before CME Globex sprang into action in June 1992, the exchange approved plans to open the upper trading floor at a cost of $26.6 million.[10] The upper trading floor, dedicated

CME traders celebrated the final day of trading on the exchange's lower trading floor with trade offers and flying papers. The 1993 move to utilize the 30,000-square-foot-plus upper trading floor, designated specifically for foreign exchange and interest rate products, proved a testament to CME's explosive growth.

CHAPTER NINE

A NEW ERA

2000–2003

We're dynamic. Thank God we're dynamic.

—Veteran CME trader and CME Board member Yra Harris

THE 21st CENTURY HERALDED A new era for Chicago Mercantile Exchange (CME). Needing to respond to competitive challenges converging from a variety of threats, including aggressive competition from European exchanges as well as the mass invasion of technology into the markets, CME was determined to address each confrontation head-on. "The house that pork bellies built" would blaze new trails in the opening years of the new century, setting standards for the industry with collaborative and original action.

In February 2000, James McNulty arrived at CME from the international investment banking firm Warburg Dillon Read. A fourth-generation Chicagoan, McNulty assumed the CEO role left open after Rick Kilcollin departed in March 1999.[1] Together with CME's Board of Directors, McNulty encountered a business fading in value under the assault of competitors and the electronic age. While membership seat prices, once reaching $900,000, fell to little over $300,000, CME members experienced concern over the exchange's future. A growing over-the-counter (OTC) derivatives business further threatened a number of CME's benchmark products.

"The OTC business was getting so big, and it looked like it was just going to eat up our short-term interest rate products. It was going to eat up some of our stock index products, and our business really started to go south in 1996, 1997, and

1998," recalled Board member Terry Duffy. "So people began to think there was a real problem."[2]

CME was not the only exchange feeling the pinch of competition and market conditions. A steady market, the frequent enemy of futures markets intent on managing price risk and inviting volatility, sent shivers through the halls of the neighboring Chicago Board of Trade (CBOT) as well. Chicago's top two exchanges needed to act—and act quickly—if Chicago was to remain the nexus of the nation's financial risk management.

"When there's stability, exchanges don't do well; when there's chaos, exchanges do very well," said Phupinder Gill, a magnetic and straightforward CME administrative leader encountering the dubious task of turning the agreement into a functioning reality. Gill met the challenge with vigor and velocity. He began running the CME clearinghouse in 1998. "Profitability of the exchanges was nonexistent [in the mid-1990s]; the revenues at the exchanges were non-

---

Pressed with the inevitable challenge of incorporating technology and electronic trading into CME's way of life, exchange leaders remained convinced that each venue—CME Globex and open outcry—had its advantages. Rather than impose a change on members, CME hierarchy allowed each venue to flourish and give customers a choice.

existent. So it led the leadership at CME, and the CBOT to begin exploring more cooperative deals."[3]

The Road to Demutualization

Beginning in the late 1990s, the CME Board began discussing the idea of demutualization, a process that would convert its membership interests into shares of common stock trading separately from exchange trading privileges. Demutualization, it was understood, would eventually lead CME into becoming a publicly traded company, something virtually unthinkable a decade prior.

"In the old days when we were formed, we were all either agriculture producers or something like that, where there was a mutuality of interest. But, as we began to branch out into financial instruments and then we moved into stock index futures, our membership base became very diverse," said Jim Oliff, CME's vice chairman. "In the world that was emerging in 1997 and 1998, it was clearly necessary to have one common pursuit, which is shareholder value, and then be able to act swiftly. That was really the motivation behind most of it."[4]

Traditionally governed by more than 100 committees, CME served as one of the nation's most democratic institutions. "There was a committee to reduce the number of committees," said Board member Bill Miller.[5] Exchange leaders increasingly came

to view the move to demutualize as a necessary one, and an important step in keeping with the times. The Board hired the consulting firm of McKinsey & Company to help develop a plan. Duffy explained:

We had to figure out new ways to do what we're going to do, and we had to decide what we wanted to look like in the future. One of the things that kept coming up was to demutualize the exchange because the European exchanges were already publicly traded.[6]

Central to the discussion of demutualization included the impending issue of technology and just how much CME would move toward becoming an electronic exchange. With a variety of European exchanges successfully pursuing their own electronic marketplaces, CME recognized its diminished role in the global economy. Any passivity on CME's part was likely to damage the decades of innovation and success that had previously allowed CME to soar.

"We were at a point where our working capital was being worked down, diminished a little bit. So we needed to make some bold decisions and really start focusing on the electronic aspects and the ability to compete globally. The Board realized that, saw it, and knew what it had to do," said Jamie Parisi, who came to CME in 1988 before rising to the role of director of planning and finance by 2000.[7]

At least on the national scene, CME would stand alone in such an endeavor. Never before had a U.S. exchange demutualized—CME would be the first, honoring its tradition of pioneering unique business initiatives. Before anything could be done, however, the CME Board needed to discern how equity would be split among its three divisions—

Left: Nobel Laureate Milton Friedman, PhD (center), toured CME's trading floor as Chairman Terry Duffy (left) followed on November 7, 2002. It was Friedman's research and credibility in the financial community that allowed CME to pursue the creation of the IMM and thereby revolutionize the world of futures trading.

Opposite: On its final day as a nonprofit exchange in 2000, traders on the CME floor celebrated amid falling confetti. The move toward demutualization was overwhelmingly supported by membership and approved on June 6, 2000.

CME, International Monetary Market (IMM), and Index and Options Market (IOM) members—all holding different stakes in the franchise.

"It seemed like we would meet every single week for months just discussing how we would do this, how we would divide the membership, how we would split up the equity," said David Gomach, CME's chief financial officer.[8]

Eventually, the Board approved the plan, giving three votes to full CME members, two to IMM seat holders, and one to IOM members. Despite the trepidation over taking such an unusual step, the Board remained convinced that this action maintained the best interests of members.

"The Board saw, at some point in time, that products are going to be traded electronically, and if we wanted to do the right thing for the membership, we needed to start moving in that direction," said Gomach.[9]

Convincing the membership, however, would prove to be an arduous task, requiring commitment from CME leaders and faith from members. Though new to the CEO office, McNulty was assigned the task of convincing membership that demutualization was CME's necessary path. To the CME leaders' surprise, the suggestion earned a standing ovation at a members' meeting—a sign of the membership's faith in its leadership.[10]

"There was a lot of finesse that was required in order to get the members to agree to a plan up front, a plan they knew would largely disenfranchise them," said John McPartland of the Federal Reserve Bank of Chicago.[11]

Just as traders had concerns over CME Globex and the doom it might spell to the sanctity of the pits, the question of demutualization prompted concerns among traders that the exchange would become too tech-heavy. The vote for demutualization, most members realized, served as an authorization to drastically increase the role of technology. "We had very limited resources in technology and a $50 million bottom line," said Duffy. "But you had to convince these guys that we needed their vote to go forward."[12]

Furthermore, demutualization would likely create a culture shift at CME. Long a place where democracy dominated and member voices were heard—in fact, an initiative championed by Leo Melamed and others in the late 1960s—CME would need to alter its way of thinking, particularly if taking the company public was to serve as a serious initiative. Gomach explained:

The culture had to change to where we reduced the number of committees from over 100 to, say, 10 or 15. The staff had to make decisions that a lot of them weren't [familiar] with. So it basically came down to deciding that we're going to start reducing costs around here. This isn't a membership, a club, an organization anymore. It's going to be a for-profit.[13]

On June 6, 2000, CME members supported the leadership's bold plan to demutualize and did so by an overwhelming 98 percent vote. In approving the plan, CME positioned itself as the nation's first exchange to become for-profit, all but guaranteeing its ability to stay competitive amid a changing financial landscape in which quick decisions were necessary for survival.

Underlying the approval of demutualization was the plan to pursue electronic trading for the first time in exchange history. While CME Globex had been running since 1992, with a second, more comprehensive version joining the roster in 1998, CME leaders understood electronic trading represented the future of the industry.

"At the time, cash was going down. We were seeing competition from the Europeans through electronic trading. So things weren't really rosy. It was a move that we thought was necessary to begin the process of pushing electronic trading, which is the key to these businesses," said John Peschier, CME's director of investor relations.[14]

The vote for demutualization has since allowed CME to respond more quickly to market demands and to capitalize more fully on the exchange's potential, particularly in the electronic trading arena. John R. Roberts, who witnessed CME's demutualization occur from his post in San Francisco with Barclays Global Investors before joining CME in 2003, commented:

Demutualized stock ownership keeps the institution focused on what's in the best interest of the shareholders. CME is an enterprise now that pro-

vides an electronic forum for buyers and sellers to meet, and it matches the trades, and guarantees the trades through CME Clearing; the exchange is very single-mindedly focused on that. With that focus and a cleaner decision-making process comes more agility. It focuses more on identifying opportunities, and I think it enables CME to execute against those opportunities faster.[15]

With demutualization, CME retained its status as one of the world's most innovative financial institutions, emboldening others to make similar moves, thereby creating a more comprehensive market environment. According to Thomas A. Russo, vice chairman and chief legal officer for Lehman Brothers:

One thing after the other, it was all pioneering. It was innovation that became the hallmark of CME, and it was innovation with all its components. Implementation. Execution. And creating a precedent that would lead to a much higher comfort level to other people doing essentially the same thing. For a major exchange to do what it did was an incredible thing; it changed the way we look at the markets. Markets suddenly became even more competitive and more results-oriented because of the demutualization.[16]

Robert Glauber, chairman and CEO of the National Association of Securities Dealers, agreed

---

After the near two-decade ban on trading of single-stock futures, CME joined with the CBOE and the CBOT in creating the OneChicago venture. CBOE leaders Mark Duffy and William J. Brodsky, former CME president, joined current CME CEO James McNulty and Chairman Scott Gordon to announce the partnership on May 6, 2001.

that CME's pioneering effort to demutualize represented a daring step in a new direction, thereby altering the course of exchanges' participation in the markets. Demutualization also provided CME with its most revolutionary step since the formation of the IMM three decades prior.

"It's an idea whose time had come, and it's a good one. It allows these institutions to raise capital, which they need if they're going to be technologically competitive," said Glauber. "The other thing it does is it imposes on them a discipline to run like a business."[17]

OneChicago

After the pioneering move to demutualize, discussions turned to CME's next major advancement into the future. In 2002, CME was in the midst of record revenues and earnings, a year that would end with a record volume of 558 million contracts and an average daily volume of 2.2 million contracts. Furthermore, CME ended 2002 with a new high in open interest, a key measure of its liquidity and strength in the market. CME Globex volume reached 198 million for the year, with daily value surpassing the $1 million mark for the first time on June 12, 2002. Globex would then go on to trade one million contracts in a day, 54 more times than on the 2002 calendar.

Two of the exchange's flagship products also reached high honors: the Eurodollar contract achieved recognition as the world's most actively traded futures contract, while its E-mini S&P 500 traded a record 116 million contracts, furthering its claim as the fastest-growing product in CME's history.[18] The year 2002 was also one of many milestones—the 30th anniversary of the IMM, the 20th anniversary of S&P 500 futures, the 10th anniversary of CME Globex, and the fifth anniversary of the wildly successful E-mini S&P 500 contract.[19]

Heading into the new century, CME identified a number of primary initiatives, including adding new products and services to address the world's current and emerging risk-management needs. In August 2002, federal regulators lifted an 18-year ban on trading single-stock futures. Seeking to gain added momentum, CME joined with its Chicago counterparts, the Chicago Board Options Exchange (CBOE) and CBOT, to launch OneChicago, a ven-

In 2002, CME leaders, traders, and guests marked the 10th anniversary of CME Globex with a formal gala at Chicago's famed Navy Pier. "Celebrating 10 Years on Electronic Trading" read the tribute to CME Globex as CME's decade-long relationship with its electronic platform emerged from a futuristic idea to a dominant role in CME's pursuit of liquidity and volume.

ture offering trading in futures on single stocks, narrow-based indexes and exchange-traded funds. Nearly 100 single-stock futures contracts would be traded by year's end.[20]

"It was something that nobody was really confident about, but it was a market that could potentially be very large," said Gomach. "Some of the people on the Board realize that products in our industry sometimes take several years to become great products, that you have to keep them on the shelf and keep nur-

Above: Occasionally, trading in the pits slowed long enough for traders to peer at the boards and observe current prices and market movement without flailing arms and booming voices challenging a moment for perspective and study.

Below: Just months after taking office in 2001, newly inaugurated United States President George W. Bush took a journey to CME's pits and was surrounded by the floor's traders.

turing them, and their time may come. And it may not, but you can't pull the plug too early. So they've kept it running, and it's profitable. But it's a new market and potentially a large market."[21]

And as history has shown for CME, getting to the market first often serves as the most important ingredient for success.

IPO Road Show

With its demutualization in 2000, CME membership recognized the institution would eventually make the move toward taking the company public. Principal in the vote to demutualize was a push toward greater utilization of technology as well as a conservative governance structure to show investors that CME was a secure investment.

"We knew to take the company public we had to show them that we had the proper disciplines and culture in place so that investors would someday say, 'Yes, I like that company.' So that was kind of happening on a concurrent path with the whole demutualization," said Gomach.[22]

While specific plans for the initial public offering (IPO) began soon after the demutualization announcement, the exchange struggled to find the right formula. Terry Duffy, who became chairman in April 2002, said:

We had our company valued at somewhere around $18 to $20 a share. We pulled our original

IPO. We didn't think that the business model was a sustainable one at the time, and we needed to shore that up.

This is during the transition from open outcry to electronic more and more, and people were looking at what we were going to sell. "What are we going to tell the investors?" Because no exchange had ever gone public before in the United States.[23]

Less than two months after the September 11 attacks, United States Marines visited the CME floor to commemorate the birthday of the armed services branch. The Marines' November 9, 2001, visit proved to be an emotional one for many CME members and traders, as many held personal connections with victims of the attacks on New York's World Trade Center.

September 11, 2001

Tragedy struck the nation, however, on September 11, 2001, as the terrorist attacks on New York and Washington, D.C., sent tremors throughout the financial world. At CME, the brokers' desks relayed accounts of the day's events to traders in the pit, most reports emerging first-hand by telephone in New York. A somber mood overwhelmed the exchange as trading in the pits and on CME Globex ceased early on September 11 and remained closed the following day.

The economy endured a plunge of its own, and the nation struggled with uncertainty and panic. After a necessary period of reflection and a search for answers, the nation's economy resumed movement. On Wacker Drive, CME leaders remained steadfast on the course of taking the franchise public. Craig Donohue, CME's chief administrative officer, said:

There was a lot of work to be done to help the analysts and investment community understand how this exchange operates, how we make money, what drives our growth in business. We also had the issues of people feeling that it would be difficult for us as a 100-year-old membership

institution to become a leading electronic exchange and, equally, that it would be difficult to make the transition from being a member-driven organization accountable to the members to being a public company accountable to public company shareholders. We had to overcome that.[24]

Friday, December 6, 2002, served as a monumental day for not only CME but also the NYSE. As the first exchange to become a publicly traded entity, CME solidified its position as an innovative leader in the financial industry, while simultaneously bringing a new type of stock to the NYSE floor.

Though most outsiders envisioned CME moving all its trading to the electronic platform, CME leaders believed both trading venues, electronic and open outcry, were necessary for success; dropping open outcry would prove a disastrous mistake. As in many times in its history, CME trusted its instincts, and the exchange forged ahead, pursuing a plan many thought impossible.

"Once we ironed out our business plan and got the [investment] bankers to understand it so they could explain it to their investors, we went on the road, and we started to preach the value of the company," said Duffy.[25]

Newly installed Chairman Terry Duffy joined CEO Jim McNulty and Chief Financial Officer David

Gomach, as well as exchange icons Leo Melamed and Jack Sandner, in journeying to boardrooms around the nation to educate the public on CME's past, current, and future success.

When investors wanted to hear about the future, CME delivered the facts. "Our open interest—it's at record levels. It's 21 million contracts when we went on the road show," Sandner said. "We're selling this exchange to investors. We're telling them about future and about growth. It's not about now and what we've done so far. It's about why should we invest now for the future— because the open interest portends our future. It's at record levels."[26]

CME's Competitive Markets Advisory Council

THE MISSION OF THE COMPETITIVE MARkets Advisory Council (CMAC) is to provide strategic recommendations to CME's Board in the form of policy, analyses, position papers, and other strategic recommendations that promote CME's competitive positioning as the preeminent exchange and clearinghouse in the global financial markets.

The membership comprises an impressive list of leaders in the field of economics and the financial arena.

- Myron S. Scholes, CMAC chairman; Nobel Prize–winning economist; chairman, Platinum Grove Asset Management
- Leo Melamed, CMAC vice chairman; chairman emeritus, CME
- Terrence A. Duffy, CMAC permanent director; Chairman of the Board, CME
- Craig S. Donohue, CMAC permanent director; CEO, CME
- Phupinder S. Gill, CMAC permanent director; president and chief operating officer, CME

- John F. Sandner, CMAC permanent director; retired chairman, CME

Current outside members include:

- Gary S. Becker, Nobel Prize–winning economist; professor of economics and sociology, University of Chicago
- John P. Gould, Steven G. Rothmeier Distinguished Service Professor of Economics; University of Chicago, Graduate School of Business
- David D. Hale, international economist and founder, Hale Advisors, LLC
- Robert C. Merton, Nobel Prize–winning economist; John and Natty McArthur University Professor, Harvard Business School
- Robert J. Shiller, Stanley B. Resor Professor of Economics, Yale University; chief economist, Macro Securities Research, LLC

Though frequent rivals, the Chicago exchanges had moved toward a more friendly relationship throughout the latter stages of the 20th century. The OneChicago venture between CME, CBOT, and CBOE further enhanced cooperation. Now, seeking a better arrangement, as well as a more collaborative relationship, Carey and Duffy championed efforts to pursue a common clearinghouse link. The chairmen recognized the potential of the deal and the advantages it would offer to each institution. Convincing the respective memberships, however, would likely prove a more arduous task as each institution possessed its own culture, attitude, and bias about the other. Yet Carey and

Duffy, along with CME Clearinghouse Director Phupinder Gill, met the challenge.

"In the end, it was the logic that became compelling. We had approached the Board of Trade, and they had approached us on many different occasions," Oliff said. "The presence of both Terry Duffy and Charlie Carey in the top seats enabled that deal to get done."[36]

On November 24, 2003, a clearing agreement between CME and CBOT began operation, thanks in large part to the long hours of Gill's clearinghouse staff, a group charged with creating the hardware to handle efficiently the trades of the world's two premier exchanges in short time. By January 4, 2004,

CME would provide clearing and settlement services for all CBOT products.[37]

"So now the Board of Trade gets a better deal, and the Merc, every time the volume of the Chicago Board of Trade grows, [it gets] more money from that," Davis said. "What happened was it became a win-win situation for the Chicago Merc, and to that extent, it became a winning situation for the Chicago Board of Trade compared to the way it was before. But there were dynamics that kept it from happening earlier."[38]

The partnership, once considered unimaginable, responded to the competitive challenge posed by Eurex and the technological wave, solidified Chicago's place as a premier financial market and created nearly $1.8 billion worth of capital efficiencies.[39] Additionally, the agreement made CME the largest derivatives clearing organization in the world.[40] "I think the clearinghouse, as it stands now, stands head and shoulders above anybody else in the entire world," said Gill, whom other CME leaders have credited with placing CME in such an envious position.[41]

In his 2003 annual remarks to shareholders, Duffy noted the scope of the agreement, saying:

This historic transaction—between the two largest futures exchanges in the United States— will give our clearing firms and customers significant operational, margin, and capital efficiencies. It exemplifies our best efforts to provide value to our customers and shareholders at the same time.[42]

The positive results of the deal have extended well beyond dollar figures. No longer is the distance between CME's Wacker Drive headquarters and the CBOT's LaSalle Street home such a cavernous divide. "Strategically, it's been a huge benefit to CME and the CBOT. Economically, we have been very blessed with that deal, and I think it's helped us to be able to talk with the Board of Trade more openly," said Duffy.[43]

Furthermore, the agreement has afforded CME added stature in even the most critical of financial circles and reinforced its commitment to making confident decisions to advance the franchise. "[The clearing agreement] was, I think, a galvanizing point with CME and its investors," said Gomach. "You go out on these road shows and you kind of say, 'Here's our history. Here's what we're going to do.' It really gets you credibility with investors."[44]

In 2003, at the initiative of Melamed and with the approval of Duffy, the CME Board authorized the creation of the CME Center for Innovation, appointing Colleen Lazar as its executive director. The center's mission is to identify, foster, and showcase examples of significant innovation and creative thinking pertaining to markets, commerce, or trade in the public and private sectors.

One of the center's early accomplishments involved the establishment of a Competitive Markets Advisory Council (CMAC) to act as an "academic think tank" by providing a forum to generate ideas and discussions pertinent to the future direction of the exchange.

CMAC members also provide leadership to advance the causes of the CME Center for Innovation through their involvement in choosing an annual recipient of the prestigious Fred Arditti Innovation Award. This award, named after the 1980s CME economist who created the specifications for the highly successful Eurodollar contract, recognizes an individual for his or her outstanding contributions to commerce, markets, and trade. William F. Sharpe, the 1990 Nobel Prize–winning economist, received the first award in 2004, while Melamed was recognized with the 2005 award.

Continuing the Pace

Beginning in 2003, under the direction of Melamed, CME adopted an "Asian strategy" in order to raise CME's visibility and presence in Asia and particularly within the People's Republic of China. As a consequence, Melamed led CME in organizing a continuous interchange of discussions and educational programs with the financial community and government officials in China.

With yet one more strategic initiative in its wake, CME continued to grow. In late 2003, the exchange launched trading in E-mini Nasdaq Composite Index futures, another way CME would offer financial managers the means to manage market risk.[45] Duffy told CME shareholders:

Our strong performance can be directly attributed to the foresight of CME's Board of Directors who, in 1998, recognized the need for us to dramatically change our business model.

Frankly, the easiest path would have been to cling to our old ways of doing business—trying to protect what we had while we could. Instead, as is typical of this organization, our members looked the future in the eye and began to change. We initiated a long, tedious, difficult, and rewarding process of reinventing our business in a way that would turn our competitive threats into new opportunities.[46]

As 2003 came to a close, McNulty left CME as its CEO, handing over the office to Donohue.

Donohue's arrival as CEO represented his steady ascent up CME's corporate ladder. His pairing with Chairman Duffy provided CME with two visionaries capable of adding momentum to the exchange. During this period of transition, Melamed served as a valuable source of advice and guidance to the Board.

Now, as a public company, CME was very transparent, making each step a visible move for shareholders, investors, members, and the entire financial world to observe.

"It's not like we're holding our cards close to our vests anymore," Duffy said. "The cards are on the table. We can all see what we're worth now."[47]

In 2004, the exchange opened its interactive CME Visitors Center in the lobby of its Wacker Drive home. The center not only tells the story of CME's evolution in narratives, pictures, video, and audio, but also provides guests the opportunity to simulate buying and selling as traders on the floor.

CHAPTER TEN

CME GLOBEX

2004–2006

We've had extraordinary growth and we are, at this point, the largest, most diverse exchange in the world.

—Craig Donohue

WITH CHICAGO MERCANTILE Exchange's (CME) arrival into the first years of the 21ˢᵗ century, the exchange continued to demonstrate its significant role in the world's financial markets for all to see. A critical component to the smooth running of the global economy, CME consistently advanced to reinvent itself and, at times, its industry.

For all of its growth and innovation, CME still relied on principles embedded within its institutional fabric. Although tremendous progress had been made, exchange leaders understood the competition would not relent, and CME sought to remain in the forefront of the world's most active exchanges.

Driving Ahead

In autumn 2003, CME opened another overseas office—this one in Sydney, Australia. By January 2004, the CME Globex platform provided Australian traders access to CME's vast markets, the first non-Australian exchange to forge such a relationship. In February 2004, CME announced the launch of Nikkei 225 stock index futures on CME Globex[1] as well as trading futures contracts on the U.S. Consumer Price Index, the first product CME ever listed on a major economic indicator.[2]

On March 4, 2004, CME opened its Globex Learning Center, the world's first training facility dedicated to electronic trading, and followed a day later with the unveiling of its interactive visitors center (containing video, touch screens, and audio in a historical documentary of CME) in the lobby of 20 South Wacker Drive. The pair of openings demonstrated the commitment and pursuit of innovation inherent in the exchange.[3]

"Chicago is where the world comes to manage risk," said CEO Craig Donohue on the eve of the opening gala event. "From a business standpoint, our creation of the Globex Learning Center and the new visitors center not only serves to boost Chicago's stature as a world financial center, but also demonstrates CME's commitment to this city."[4]

To become a more active force in the European market, CME provided a CME Globex pricing incentive program for 18 months beginning in November 2003. The move, which slashed electronic trading transaction fees, sought to increase CME's presence

---

In 2003, the Globex Learning Center opened on Wacker Drive. It was created as a venue to bridge the gap successfully between open-outcry trading and electronic trading. Spearheaded by the efforts of the exchange's Electronic Trading Committee, the center replicates an electronic trading room, while offering trading courses, mock sessions, and seminars.

The advancement of CME's electronic trading platform, CME Globex, has allowed the exchange to evolve from a midwestern financial institution into a global leader defying both geography and time. Here, Vice Chairman Jim Oliff (left) joined Chairman Terry Duffy in the Globex Learning Center, detailing for guests the scope of the system's operations.

in Europe and spread the use of CME Globex abroad.[5] By June 2004, CME would waive transaction fees for new traders utilizing the CME Globex system, a move designed to attract additional market participants.[6]

Seeking a presence in China, anticipated as the world's next emergent marketplace, CME announced its partnership with the Shanghai Futures Exchange (SHFE) on March 18, 2004. CME leaders acknowledged that the move placed them in a strong position to capitalize on that region's continued economic growth.[7]

The next day, CME announced the formation of its Competitive Markets Advisory Council (CMAC). A think tank assembled to develop and analyze market policies and issues, the CMAC included three Nobel Prize winners—Myron S. Scholes, Gary S. Becker, and Robert C. Merton—in addition to University of Chicago Professor John P. Gould and international economist David D. Hale. CME mainstays Leo Melamed and Jack Sandner also joined current exchange leaders Terry Duffy

and Donohue on the council. Long an industry pioneer, the creation of the CMAC sought to be a recognized forum for independent thought and the discussion of competitive market issues.[8]

In May, CME joined with a former partner, Reuters, in offering CME's Globex foreign exchange market to sell side traders in the interbank foreign exchange market. In creating a more efficient and dynamic marketplace, CME not only continued its path of adding value for shareholders, but also staked its claim in capturing a more significant portion of the $500 billion traded in foreign exchange each day.[9] The agreement with Reuters followed on the heels of expanded electronic trading hours. As CME Globex volume continued to shoot upward (trading 1.6 million contracts per day by April 2004), demand for the electronic platform urged CME to extend its working hours over the 23-hour mark, making the CME Globex workday the longest of the world's major future exchanges.[10]

The Electronic Eurodollar

With increasing vigor, CME focused on CME Globex, recognizing that the future promise of the exchange rested very much on the success of its electronic platform. With its infusion into European markets, as well as the Asian and Australian continents, CME leaders would look to the exchange's benchmark product, the Eurodollar, to take CME Globex and CME to the next level.

In the early months of 2004, CME faced direct competition from the London International Financial Futures and Options Exchange (LIFFE). LIFFE planned to release its own Eurodollar contract, a near replica of CME's hallmark product, and to do so solely on an electronic platform. With the financial world gravitating toward PC trading and the bulk of Eurodollar trading at CME conducted through open outcry on Wacker Drive, LIFFE's action served as a clear threat to CME business.

In response, CME leaders readied a proposal for Class B shareholders of CME stock. The proposal would allow the CME Board of Directors to list the first two months of the Eurodollar contract on CME Globex, but only if trading failed to achieve defined numbers on the floor. After the shareholders' unanimous approval on March 16, two days before LIFFE's Eurodollar contract sprang to electronic life, CME's Eurodollar volume began to rise. By the end of March, activity on CME Globex surpassed open-outcry volume for the first time in CME history.[11]

Less than a month after the vote, CME Globex trading of the Eurodollar jumped to 17 percent of the contract's total volume—a significant leap from the 7 percent of Eurodollars traded electronically just three months prior in January. The spring in electronic trading of the Eurodollar helped elevate the contract to more than the two-million-per-day mark, an all-time high for the exchange.[12]

From summer to fall 2004, CME retained a 98 percent total of Eurodollar contracts traded globally and claimed 98 percent of all open interest in the contract, while trading nearly 1.8 million Eurodollar contracts per day.[13] The explosion of Eurodollar trading on CME Globex aided the growing numbers as 60 percent of all Eurodollar contracts shifted hands electronically.[14] Duffy told CNN in September 2004:

When you look at our business, you can see that we've grown rapidly with electronic trading. Just look at our largest contract in the world, our Eurodollar complex—it was only 15 percent electronic in January. Today, we're averaging roughly 70 percent electronic. So we are growing leaps and bounds on the electronic venue here at CME in our largest products.[15]

One Billion Times

For the first time in its history, trading on the CME Globex platform surpassed open outcry in a one-quarter period. CME Globex trading in the second quarter of 2004 accounted for 52 percent of the exchange's increasing volume.[16] Long predicted as the exchange's most promising instrument for the future, Globex arrived as a major player in CME's arsenal as electronic business refused to slow.

On October 19, 2004, the CME Globex electronic trading platform recorded its one billionth trade. For a system once stalled in delays and inefficiencies, a system comprehensively revised in the early 1990s, CME Globex had finally hurdled its once problematic past in driving the exchange atop the world's economic landscape. As the futures world became one connected by milliseconds and

mouse clicks, CME found itself benefiting from the developments.

"When you can take an electronic product and you can disseminate it throughout the world versus at 20 South Wacker, well obviously, you're going to trade at a hell of a lot more volume to make a hell of a lot more money," said Duffy of CME Globex's influence and force in CME business.[17]

As 2004 came to a close, CME reported another year of record numbers. Trading volume reached 787 million contracts, a 27 percent jump from 2003, with a national trading value of $463 trillion. Open interest totaled 22.5 million contracts, while electronic trading, a point of emphasis for the exchange, soared to capture 70 percent of CME's total volume.[18]

In his annual remarks to shareholders, Duffy characterized CME's explosive growth as a matter of swift and efficient action:

In every situation where our competitive position has been challenged, CME has responded quickly and effectively. We continue to provide our customers with unparalleled advantages of liquidity, transparency, and efficiency.[19]

Where the Exchange Has Been …

Since its inception in 1898 as a modest butter and egg exchange, Chicago Mercantile Exchange has survived threatening competition, government intervention, near extinction, cynics questioning its moves and motives, and the formation of a global economy shunning both geography and time.

"The Chicago Mercantile Exchange, once the house that pork bellies built, is today the house that innovation built," said Leo Melamed. "The transactions that CME clears are a direct consequence of the innovations our exchange undertook, the intellectual capital we invested, the time we devoted, and the money we spent on research, development, education, and marketing. All of which begot us the crown jewel of the marketplace: liquidity."[20]

The launch of financial futures, the idea of cash settlement, and CME Globex have all served as pioneering events for CME, helping to elevate the exchange to the global status it enjoys today.

LIFE IN THE PITS

AS CHICAGO MERCANTILE EXCHANGE (CME) and similar institutions across the nation move toward electronic trading, the traditions of open outcry have begun fleeting. While some exchanges have ended pit trading in favor of electronic platforms altogether, CME has remained content to let customers decide. Despite the exchange's booming volume, increased attention, and investment in technology, action in the pits has not faltered. Ultimately, CME leaders argue, the customers and the market will decide.

"We took a different approach than the European exchanges did when they went electronic," said Jamie Parisi, CME's chief financial officer. "They said they were going to turn off their floor on a given day and transition to electronic. We said, 'No, they're both viable markets.'"[1]

The pits, however, remain CME's defining feature—a vibrant whirl of voices, limbs, and colors capturing imaginations—and contain many of the exchange's most intriguing characters and stories. Despite concerns that the pits would face a quick end with the launch of CME Globex and demutualization, open-out-cry action on Wacker Drive has not settled. CME Board member Patrick Lynch said:

It is one of the purest forms of capitalism you could have because it's you against, in essence, the market. There's a report card that comes out daily, even hourly, every minute.[2]

Martin Callaghan, who spent more than three decades in the hog pits since joining CME in 1970, said the pits remain stable with a healthy combination of consistency and self-policing.

"People that started with the livestock, even though there were other markets to trade, they kind of stayed with them. You could develop a trading strategy for the next hour, the next day, the next month, and I never left, and I know a lot of guys that didn't," Callaghan said. "There is a certain unwritten set of rules that we stand by. We won't let guys get out of line if we think they're doing something shady. We try to help each other out as far as if a guy is in trouble, and it's always been that way. If a guy gets out of line, everyone lets him know, and he will feel the consequences if he doesn't toe the line."[3]

Today, the pits remain much as they were a decade ago—a culture all their own with their own language and unique set of clothing and customs: red jackets for members, yellow jackets for traders of member institutions, gold badges for CME members, and green badges for IMM members.[4]

Regardless of the commodity, each pit has its superstars, veteran players, and rookies. At the end of the day, traders can be tired but fried—a successful day; or burnt—a negative day. Some may be mooches—taking advantage of others' trading errors; while others may be carps—slow traders who merely

repeat the shouts of others. The best-case scenario for the day may be a "hit and run," when enough money is made in the morning to head home early.[5]

The pits shriek of risk-taking and competition, albeit in a friendly environment where tempers flare but grudges rarely last. Although one trader once described the pits as "an arena of low brows and low blows."[6] Like those who hustled to the California Gold Rush, the pits lure the most ambitious of capitalists. In its early days and into the 1970s, the pits could serve a stable career; with the explosion of the markets in the 1980s and 1990s—Eurodollars, E-mini, electronic trading, stock options— the pits often created big winners and losers; indeed, the pits emerged the place for both heroes and goats.

Some reach their end with a fundamentalist style, scouring the news to make their decisions based on what they see. Others, meanwhile, claim a technician's approach—watching price movements in the pits and responding to what's happening in the present moment.[7] Almost all traders rely on hints of instinct and emotion. Yet, as traders trek from agricultural pits to Treasury pits, the spirit remains intact regardless of one's tactics—free enterprise knows no boundaries.

Tales of self-destruction are neither uncommon nor infrequent. While some can take their millions and head into early retirement, many elect to stay and continue to challenge the market's wisdom and wrath. Indeed, the smartest traders know one cannot beat the market, pushing ego aside when one has lost. Lynch explained:

> You have to be willing to accept that you're going to be wrong quite a bit. From being down here so long, you see the people who don't make it. And it's not what they do with their winners, it's what they do with their losers.[8]

That maxim can apply just as equally to the traders who fill their time in front of computer screens, the more dominant method these days.

For traders in the pits reluctant to abandon the open-outcry sessions, CME introduced a handheld trading device in 1999. Called Galax-C, the handheld unit has allowed many traders to merge the immediate pulse of market action with the orderliness of electronic trading.

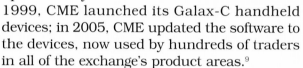

Some pit-traders have merged the old with the new by using handheld PCs to trade electronically, while simultaneously shifting contracts in open-outcry sessions. In 1999, CME launched its Galax-C handheld devices; in 2005, CME updated the software to the devices, now used by hundreds of traders in all of the exchange's product areas.[9]

Still, many traders have refused to desert the traditional pit method altogether. Although electronic trading offers anonymity, speed, and reliability on the order execution, it lacks in dispersing the energy of the market. Some electronic traders, in fact, sit at their PC with earphones on that mimic the noises of the pits. For so long the pulse of the markets beat inside the pits, though electronic trading has become the day's leading system. That beat inside the pit continues, and traders like to feel its push— the facial expressions, intonations, and movements of fellow traders seizing the market's ascent or fall.

While CME leaders acknowledge that users will decide when open outcry ceases, its fading importance in the face of technology has not written its end to date. CME's most spirited form of capitalism continues onward, creating new characters, lingo, and stories each day.

"Yeah, we still exist here," said Callaghan, "and there's a purpose for us. Come, trade, and watch us, and give us a look, too."[10]

Indeed, the creation of the International Monetary Market (IMM) ushered in the concept of trading the ultimate commodity—money—while cash settlement opened the gates to trading indexes on everything from stocks to weather. CME Globex, meanwhile, pushed CME out of Chicago and into the world. "That is the essence of our success and the direction of the world," said Melamed.[21]

CME continues to capture the financial world's imagination and attention. From the E-mini, one of the industry's fastest-growing futures products, to the S&P 500 contract, the world's most successful equity contract, and Eurodollars, the world's most actively traded contract, CME has pioneered financial instruments helping the world move forward.[22]

"At the Merc, we literally touched every quadrant of interest rates, of fixed income with the Eurodollar contract ... stock index futures where we completely dominated the landscape, and then our own commodity space," said Todd Petzel, former CME chief economist.[23]

Truth be told, not all of CME's contracts have flourished; yet Chicago's premier exchange has never shied from the possibilities. Innovation continues to sprout from Wacker Drive, each contract nurtured to reach its potential.

"The great thing in our business is there's never a shortage of ideas," said Rick Redding, CME's managing director of products and services. "It's more a question of which ones do we think the timing is right on; which ones have the necessary characteristics to work? Some of the most successful products didn't work for a number of years. People have forgotten that Eurodollars, the largest product that's out there right now, took a couple of years before anyone noticed."[24]

For so long an institution mired in controversy and questioning, CME remains one of many exchanges benefiting from a more comprehensive public understanding of the futures markets. And it has accepted the industry's evolution, embracing the changing times to find business ideas that work. Michael Moscow, president and CEO of the Federal Reserve Bank of Chicago, explained:

CME has been successful in identifying the needs that its customers have and serving those needs, and evolving as the industry and the

Leo Melamed (left) joined CME Chairman Terry Duffy (right) in honoring Fred Arditti (center) with the CME Center for Innovation Award in 2003 and subsequently naming the award in his honor. It was Arditti's pioneering cash-settlement idea for the Eurodollar contract that allowed the once-unthinkable concept to arrive on the CME's boards.

markets changed. This is the mark of any good business. You can't sit still. The environment is always changing, and you've got to adapt to that changing environment—and CME has done it extremely well.[25]

There resides much credit to be shared. Consider the early butter and egg dealers who continued operation each day in the shadow of the Chicago Board of Trade (CBOT) and survived charges that CME was little more than a gambling den; Everette B. Harris' decision to place frozen pork bellies on the board; Leo Melamed's inventiveness to trade foreign currencies; Jack Sandner symbolizing the exchange's free enterprise spirit; and the current day's leaders, Terry Duffy and Craig Donohue, guiding the exchange in its transformation from private club to public company.

"I have always been impressed with the leadership of Chicago Mercantile Exchange," said for-

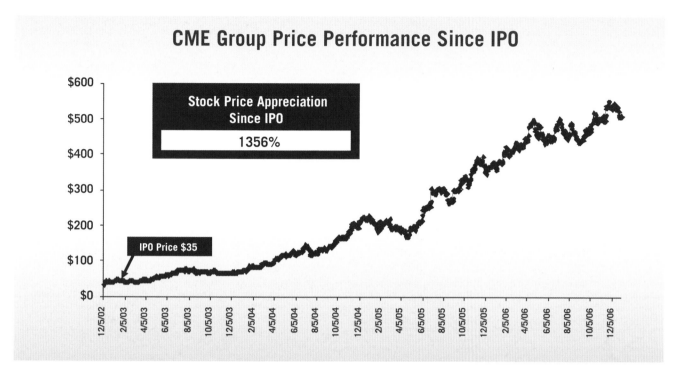

CME Group Price Performance Since IPO

Stock Price Appreciation Since IPO

1356%

IPO Price $35

Since its initial public offering in 2002, CME's stock price has appreciated by 1,356 percent.

mer U.S. Congressman and Secretary of Agriculture Dan Glickman. "The innovation and markets, its understanding of the nature of globalization, electronic markets, I think led me to believe that they were the real innovators in this new world of derivatives and futures."[26]

The exchange's far-reaching growth in the years since its demutualization and initial public offering (IPO), meanwhile, can be shared among a varied Board of Directors with decades of industry expertise, vested interest in CME's success, and an entrepreneurial hunger that refuses to subside.

"I look at our deep domain expertise we have with our Board of Directors today," said Duffy, "and I think it's a big reason why this company has been able to grow almost tenfold since its IPO. They understand the business. We're not inside/outside type directors. We're a Board working with our management in a cohesive way to deliver value for our shareholders."[27]

Board member Bill Miller noted, "There are a lot of questions and answers at our Board meetings. There's no rubber stamping. That's the nature of the Board."[28]

CME continues to forge ahead, its work far from over. John Peschier, CME's director of investor relations, observed:

The growth has really taken place here as we've shifted the culture from being a member-oriented, very slow, very hard to get decisions-made [company] into a high-flying public company. One thing about our culture here is that we're never satisfied with the status quo, and we're not going to look at our current products as cash cows. We're going to come up with new ideas.[29]

What the Future Holds

Taking a heritage redolent with dynamic thought and competitive vigor and combining it with the present day's pools of liquidity, open interest, worldwide telecommunication hubs, money in reserve, and an electronic trading system gaining users by the day, Chicago Mercantile Exchange has positioned itself for the years to come. In April 2005, CME announced its intention to dual list its stock on the NASDAQ stock market, a move prompted to provide shareholders with additional benefits.[30] Adjunct to that agreement was a plan to release the E-mini NASDAQ biotechnology index futures contracts, the first

futures contracts designed specifically for the biotech sector.[31]

In the wake of Hurricane Katrina and the devastation it caused across the nation's Gulf Coast, CME's position as a risk-management tool, a place to collect the world's volatility, emerged clear. On September 1, 2005, the day after Katrina struck, CME reported the busiest day in its history as volume topped 10.7 million contracts, nearly 70 percent of which came through CME Globex transactions.[32] With the nation and world searching for ways to manage risk, CME remained an active marketplace.

Indeed, the exchange's 2005 year-end statistics display the institution's breadth and volume. CME trades nearly 100 million contracts each month, almost three-quarters of which run through CME Globex. In October 2005 alone, CME traded nearly 4.5 million contracts each day.[33] The year closed with trading volume topping one billion contracts valued at $638 trillion, a 35 percent jump from 2004. CME Globex continued its assertive influence as well, trading 772 million contracts in 2005, a 65 percent leap from the previous year. As of December 30, 2005, CME had nearly 70 million positions of open interest.[34]

"We're fortunate that there were a lot of really smart, visionary people before us who made a lot of very good decisions that have allowed us to continue to build on that success over the last two to three years," Donohue told *Stocks, Futures and*

Options magazine in December 2005. "We're trying to make sure that this remains part of the DNA of the company."[35]

A Model Exchange

Since its 2002 IPO sold at $35 per share, CME's stock value has soared in subsequent years, one of nine U.S. companies with stock trading for more than $300 a share at the end of 2005.[36] The dramatic and near-unthinkable increase has prompted other U.S. exchanges to travel an identical path.

"What we're doing has become, I think, a model for others to emulate, and it's not at all unexpected that other financial marketplaces are going to begin doing what we started five or six years ago," Donohue told the *Chicago Tribune* in April 2005, referring to CME's demutualization, transition into a public company, and emphasis on electronic trading.[37]

A large part of CME's rapid success resides in its infrastructure. Not only does CME have unique products with global significance, but it also boasts an efficient clearinghouse that further increases capital. Few other exchanges can claim such efficiencies.

"The Merc is in an enviable position, and it's gotten there because it does have not only the trading vehicle but also the clearing vehicle. You know, CME just outsmarted the competition," said Hans Stoll, the Walker Professor of Finance at Vanderbilt University.[38]

Furthermore, CME has consistently resisted a complacent attitude. While recognizing the institution's worldwide prominence and near dominance in key product areas, exchange leaders have continuously encouraged creative energy. For CME to remain at its zenith, innovation must persist.

"Once you establish a pool of liquidity in a product, it's very difficult for anybody to break into that unless there is some inefficiency," said James

Parisi, chief financial officer for CME. "So the area of competition isn't so much on existing products as it is on innovation of new products and getting products out to market."[39]

The exchange has also pursued proactive endeavors in today's competitive climate. Even before the September 11 terrorist attacks paralyzed much of the economic business running out of New York City, CME was preparing for a potential disaster. The exchange has two undisclosed locations that run electronic trading, thereby eliminating the threat of business closing if the Wacker Drive building were to be affected. In addition, CME boasts an extensive array of backup power stations, each one anticipating a wide range of issues that could disable the regular flow of business. "We've just always been kind of focused on that in terms of making sure we're just a little bit ahead of the next guy in our thinking about things," Donohue said.[40]

For all of its accomplishments, however, some have criticized CME's lack of investment in new acquisitions in recent years while cash continues to flow into Wacker Drive. Exchange leaders maintain that they will not be rushed into a deal merely for the sake of making a deal. Leaders contend that any merger or acquisition must hold sound business initiative for the franchise. For more than

Above: Leo Melamed (right) accepted the 2005 Fred Arditti Innovation Award at an event in April 2006. Left to right: Terry Duffy, Myron Scholes, Craig Donohue, and Tom Russo. *(Photo by © David R. Barnes)*

Below: CME has acknowledged its stance today as an applied technology company as much as an exchange. The influx of technology on the floor and the advent of electronic trading has made computers as much a part of the CME culture as the traders themselves.

a century, CME has survived and flourished by adhering to its own conscience, much as many of the traders have remained on the floor, and refused to tremble in the face of critique.

"We've created a $12 billion company, even though in some people's minds it wouldn't be the poster child for corporate governance," said Donohue. "So the results speak for themselves."[41]

The Unrelenting Drive of CME Globex

While the inner sanctum of open-outcry sessions continues to be CME's most identifiable feature to outsiders and perhaps the exchange's most sacred ground, leaders have nevertheless acknowledged the fact that electronic trading represents the future. And the exchange has acted aggressively, investing nearly $1 billion in technology since the late 1990s.[42] Of the 1,300 CME employees in 2005, more than half are involved with technology, a dramatic shift even from the year 2000 when CME had less than 150 information technologists.[43]

"We've transformed our culture; we've transformed our way of thinking," said David Prosperi, CME's director of public relations. "The focus on our employee base is really finding more 'technologists,' as we call them, to help us drive the business going forward."[44]

With electronic trading systems running exchanges around the globe, CME has placed an important emphasis on staying at the top. For CME Chief Information Officer Jim Krause, who calls speed of light his worst enemy, the exchange will continue to focus on speed and reliability, the components that will keep traders utilizing CME Globex while simultaneously bringing new entrants into the system.

"Customer satisfaction is sort of the key," he said. "What's key to customer satisfaction is speed and reliability. In other words, traders either click the mouse, hit the key, do whatever they do. They know what's going to happen, and they want to get their answer fast. 'I got the trade; I got it at this price.' "[45]

Its focus on technology, meanwhile, has led to a shift in CME's outlook. Leaders contend that CME is shedding its exchange label. The push of technology, in fact, has all but determined a new perception both inside and outside its doors. Phupinder Gill, CME's president and chief operating officer, said:

The biggest area of focus for the company has been and will continue to be technology. For better or worse, we're an applied technology firm because, at the end of the day, you have a product that can trade, a customer base that's willing to trade. They're not going to come unless the technology you have supports what they want to do.[46]

Continued Evolution

"I think the big objective that we have here is where do we want CME to be positioned five years or 10 years from now, and to my way of thinking, we want to be positioned as a global financial services company," said Prosperi. "I don't think we want to be seen merely as an exchange. I think we want to be seen as an international company that provides a variety of services. Trading may be one part. Leveraging the clearing mechanism that we have here may be another part. There may be other initiatives that we haven't developed yet."[47]

James Oliff provided an electronic trading demonstration to Chinese officials in the exchange's Globex Learning Center.

Looking at CME in late 2006, many investors championed its potential—a high-margin business with room to grow, predictable revenues each year, dominance in key product lines, history of innovation and action, and more than $800 million in reserve.[48] Rumors swirled of a potential CME merger or acquisition.

"The world is getting smaller, and there's going to be more consolidation with fewer exchanges trading all the commodities around the clock," predicted Steve Newcom, a trader in CME's agricultural pits since 1977.

In fact, on the back of a rumored merger between CME and CBOT in June 2005, one prompted by CBOT officials' vague statement of a proposed acquisition or sale, CME stock rose nearly 13 percent and crossed the $300 mark.[49] Earlier, similar activity occurred in November 2004 as unfounded talk of a partnership between CME and NYSE spread and subsequently elevated CME stock over the $200 line.[50] Such activity further signified investor confidence in the CME franchise.

CME has extended its reach abroad in 2006 as well. As Asian markets expanded and attracted western participation, CME responded by opening the S&P Asia 50 index futures contract in the first quarter of 2006, continuing CME's tradition of getting to markets early and often with unique products.

"With the economic revolution that's going on in India, China, Thailand, and Singapore ... business leaders have to look out and evaluate the vision, and make a bet on the future, and again evolve and adapt," said A. Robert Abboud, a former IMM Board member.[51]

Recognizing the advancement of globalization, CME leaders have duly noted the added potential of their markets and products. As nations and economies continue to become connected in spite of geography and time, CME holds the keys to even further progress on the worldwide stage.

With customers around the world, a diverse product line, deep liquid markets, around-the-clock trading on a single platform, and strategic alliances with other exchanges—CME is truly a global marketplace.

"It's not only growth in the United States but growth worldwide," said Parisi. "As people have to borrow more, and are more affected by interest rates and cross-border transactions, they're more

Above: On December 6, 2002, Chicago Mercantile Exchange made history as it became the first publicly traded financial exchange in the United States. Since its initial IPO of $35, exchange shares had skyrocketed to prices nearing $400 in early 2006.

Below: Newly appointed Federal Reserve Chairman Ben Bernanke visited CME for a private roundtable discussion with CME leadership on June 15, 2006. Pictured left to right: Craig Donohue, Ben Bernanke, and Terry Duffy.
(Photo by © David R. Barnes)

TODAY'S CME LEADERS

*S*TOCKS, *FUTURES AND OPTIONS* MAGAzine named Terry Duffy and Craig Donohue as its 2005 Co-Persons of the Year, a fitting honor for the individuals charged with leading CME through its pioneering times. Duffy and Donohue have spearheaded the exchange's multilayered team effort and witnessed the CME franchise emerge a global leader and the envy of many.

A former agricultural trader, Duffy gained the chairman's post in April 2002 while the exchange pursued its dramatic revitalization consisting of demutualization and the initial steps of becoming a public company. In 2004, Donohue assumed the title of CEO, joining Duffy to head up an institution in the midst of rapid growth and changing times. The pair's leadership has proven to be instrumental in guiding CME through a revolutionary period in the exchange's history as well as the industry's.

Donohue, who started at CME as an attorney in 1989, found that his immersion in the CME culture in the late 1980s prompted him to consider the exchange's far-reaching possibilities. In many ways, those early ideas laid the foundation for his future as exchange leader. In 2004, Donohue told the *Chicago Tribune*:

In 1988, the CME was grappling with competitive challenges from deregulation, rapid advances in technology, and globalization of our business. I became intrigued with how a more aggressive approach to strategy execution and business development could revitalize the CME's growth prospects. Taking the business forward—becoming entrepreneurial, taking on lots of responsibilities—forever changed me.[1]

Donohue's confident attitude has transferred to other CME staff members, emboldening them to continue the exchange's forward momentum.

"Craig has been very balanced in his approach. He had inspired everybody to just go out there, do things that make sense for us," said Phupinder Gill. "He sets the tone, the tone at the top, which is basically to take some risk."[2]

Duffy's credibility in the pits as well as with investors has furthered CME's development. His savvy nature helped secure the common clearing agreement established with the CBOT in 2004, a deal that has added depth and diversity to the CME franchise. His aggressive spirit, meanwhile, has directed the exchange through both its demutualization and IPO.

"Terry was the right person at the right time," said CME Vice Chairman Jim Oliff. "He has a magnificent working relationship with every single Board member, and he is extremely well-respected by the floor."[3]

As Donohue and Duffy, both native Chicagoans, continue to lead CME through the opening decade of the 21st century, they do so representing the exchange's character as well as its innovation-charged history.

CEO Craig Donohue (left) and CME Executive Chairman Terry Duffy are the pair charged with leading CME into the 21st century. Duffy, the veteran agricultural trader in the pits, assumed the chairman's role in April 2002, while Donohue, former executive vice president and chief administrative officer at CME, became CEO in January 2004.

affected by foreign exchange rates. It's just natural that our market is going to grow as well as they go to hedge those transactions."[52]

In character typical of the one-time butter and egg exchange, exchange leaders realize that capturing increased global business will require hard work. With CME Globex paving the way, however, CME maintains a leading edge in the industry.

As such, the CME Globex electronic platform continues to define the cutting edge of financial trading technology. The functionality and capacity of the platform have grown dramatically to accommodate increased demand. CME Globex offers access to all major asset classes, including a full range of interest rate, equity index, foreign exchange, commodity, and energy and real estate products.

"We've got a lot more missionary work to do in terms of building the brand in Europe or building the brand in Asia, but those markets are absolutely open to us now," said CME Chief Marketing Officer John R. Roberts. "We're now open for business all the time, and they can trade when they want to trade."[53] CME Board member Myron Scholes, a former Nobel Prize winner, adds:

The world is becoming closer through communication and telecommunication. You have China, India, massive populations, and massive new growth in technology. Through the interactions of the futures markets, the clearing corporation, [CME] will be able to move into the 21st century running as opposed to having to rebuild everything themselves. That means a great growth potential for the Merc and its transaction acumen in addition to its ability to innovate.[54]

New products will also be a prominent feature of CME's future, honoring the institution's long-held tradition of pioneering rather than following, of innovating rather than imitating. "Most of what we're doing here is on the basis of our own inventiveness," said Donohue. "We're still not much of a follower in that sense. Most of the new things that get done emanate here. That's just something we're trying to perpetuate."[55]

While traditional thought says volatility in the marketplace allows CME to continue its burgeoning ways, exchange leaders recognize that the market does encounter its stable periods; as

CME TRUST

IN 1969, UNDER THE DIRECTION OF ITS chairman, Leo Melamed, Chicago Mercantile Exchange created the CME Trust to provide financial protection to customers in the event that a member of CME was unable to meet his or her financial obligations to a customer. Given that no CME customer has ever suffered losses due to a member's adverse financial condition, in 2005, the Trust sought and received confirmation from the Illinois Circuit Court enabling it to make charitable contributions of the net income of the CME Trust.

The CME Trust leadership subsequently decided that it would make charitable contributions to enhance economic opportunity, health, and well-being through education, while preserving the Trust's original purpose. Terry Duffy, Craig Donohue, Leo Melamed, Jack Sandner, William Miller II, Jim Oliff, and Howard Siegel were named trustees of the charitable program.

In 2006, the trustees adopted a mission statement and awarded the first grants. The trustees expect to make grants twice annually, in June and December.

The CME Trust's charitable mission supports nonprofit organizations, primarily in the Chicago region, to strengthen teaching and learning specific to financial markets, futures, and derivatives; to improve the education of disadvantaged children and youth; and to promote the health and well-being of children.[1]

such, CME must create products to handle such calm times. "In our world, we want volatility; we thrive on active markets, conflicting opinions," said John Peschier, CME's director of investor relations. "But we don't live on volatility alone, because we're going out there, and we're attracting new customers. We're rolling out new products so that we're able to overcome, to some degree, volatility."[56]

Above: Henry Paulson, Jr., secretary of the U.S. Treasury (right), received a tour of CME courtesy of Terry Duffy on August 11, 2006. *(Photo by © David R. Barnes)*

Below: Terry Duffy observed while Vice President Dick Cheney delivered a national televised economic address to Chicago business leaders and the media at CME on June 23, 2006. *(Photo by © David R. Barnes)*

A Deal on the Horizon

Meanwhile, maintaining the company's history of innovation, as well as its entrepreneurial edge, served an added source of motivation for CME leaders. Sitting still is not an option. "Coming up with innovative products and ideas"

sits atop the current CME agenda, said Rick Redding. "If you look back at the history of CME, there are a lot of firsts and a lot of things they've done. That's the only way to continue to grow the business."[57]

In recent years, CME constructed a portfolio of patents and intellectual property rights in product lines, clearing, and technology. The exchange's inventive spirit has not been sidetracked by success. According to Donohue:

That's one way we can not only preserve the integrity of our own innovations from the perspective of exploiting value, but it's also a way in which we can make money through licensing our intellectual property to other people. That also is part of the DNA of the whole company.[58]

Ultimately, leaders recognized, CME's growth potential resided in a continued record of creating an efficient place for traders and companies to manage their risk. With its liquid markets and dominance in key product areas, CME helped trading volume around the world reach new highs.

"We think more trade is better for everybody, because it makes deeper pools of liquidity and gives everybody an opportunity to hedge their risk in the most cost-effective way. So anytime you can create efficiencies in the marketplace, we think it actually adds to the trade," Duffy said.[59]

No longer hog butcher to the world, Chicago had emerged as a financial powerhouse due in large part to CME's rapid ascent; the city's once sleepy exchange, the forgotten brethren to the neighboring CBOT, was no longer an institution reliant on pork bellies. Today's CME is fast-paced and mobile, optimistic and opportunistic—the Eurodollar and the E-mini, CME Globex, and global all at once.

"Chicago clearly is the center for human capital and knowledge in this sector, and the Mercantile Exchange is an important part of that," said Michael Moscow of the Federal Reserve Bank of Chicago. "Chicago has gone through this transformation from being a manufacturing center years ago to becoming a city with a very diversified economy these days."[60]

Armed with an aggressive spirit toward progress and still a thing or two to prove to the world, CME

CME GLOBEX VOLUME GROWS

MORE THAN $1.9 TRILLION IN FUTURES and options flow through CME Globex every day. Its marketplace continues to grow and accounts for more than 70 percent of average daily futures volume executed at CME.

Through 2006, 956 million contracts, with a notional value of more than $491 trillion, have traded on CME Globex. In addition, the average daily volume of contracts rose to 3.8 million per day, which exceeded the volume of any other futures exchange. A record of 8.03 million contracts traded in a single day on CME Globex in 2006.

Noteably, the daily notional value of CME E-mini S&P 500 futures traded on CME Globex exceeds the daily notional value of all individual equity securities traded on the New York Stock Exchange.[1]

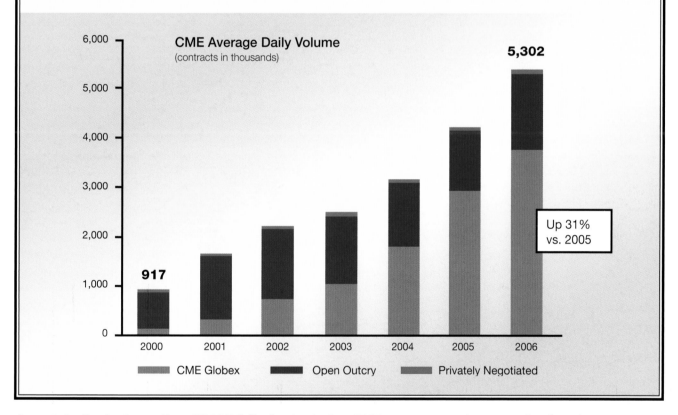

CME Average Daily Volume
(contracts in thousands)

917

5,302

Up 31% vs. 2005

CME Globex   Open Outcry   Privately Negotiated

drove into the last months of 2006 full of potential and vigor. In the hands of Terry Duffy and Craig Donohue, the exchange continued its run to life atop the financial world. Its agricultural history tucked in its vest, traders still shouting pork belly and hog orders on the Wacker Drive trading floor, CME represents a cutting-edge franchise powering into the 21st century.

And in the wings, another monumental move continued taking shape, one that would redefine the city's landscape and make headlines throughout the financial world.

Standing atop the CBOT's iconic building is Ceres, the goddess of grain and harvest. Designed by sculptor John H. Stoors, Ceres has crowned the CBOT's building since its construction in 1930 and stands as a symbolic tribute to the agricultural commodities that have long-served the CBOT well.

CHAPTER ELEVEN

THE HISTORY OF THE CHICAGO BOARD OF TRADE

There's still a tremendous motivation to innovate because if you don't innovate in this marketplace, you run the risk of becoming irrelevant. So innovation is really meeting the needs of the customers and bringing new products to the marketplace. That's the innovation, and the Board of Trade has been innovating since 1848 as well as the Merc since its start in 1874.

—Charles P. Carey

AS LATE AS OCTOBER 10, 2006, media accounts told of speculated mergers spearheaded by Chicago Mercantile Exchange (CME); those same reports also dropped another heavyweight Chicago name into the conversation—the Chicago Board of Trade (CBOT). It was rumored that CME would pair with Germany's Deutsche Boerse AG while the CBOT investigated a potential partnership with the London Metals Exchange.[1]

Yet, a week later, the official announcement of at least one merger finally broke—even if it was not the one the media had reported just days earlier. The long-rumored merger of CME and the CBOT, described by some as little more than happy hour chatter for decades, had finally turned from fiction into fact. The longtime intracity rivals, industry heavyweights but never direct product competitors, were joining forces to create the globe's largest, most diverse commodities exchange. It was a historic moment urging many to imagine the reach and influence of this new, combined financial powerhouse. The merger also sparked a look into the past, a reflection upon what brought the CBOT, long Chicago's more recognized exchange, into an agreement with CME.

A Historic Legacy

On April 3, 1848, a group of 83 Chicago merchants gathered at 101 South Water Street, in the heart of the city's bustling marketplace, and founded the CBOT, the nation's third such institution and Chicago's first commodities exchange. The group then elected Thomas Dyer as its first president, setting the stage for one of Chicago's most influential institutions. In 1851, with the exchange claiming a group of 38 full members, the CBOT processed a "forward" contract of 3,000 bushels of corn, the earliest such agreement. Quickly, the idea of forward contracts gained appeal among merchants and processors, an assurance to each group of price and delivery. A year later, the exchange moved to the intersection of Clark Street and South Water Street, remaining near the flurry of the South Water Street marketplace.

By the end of 1856, an additional 122 members would enter the CBOT's doors, this time moved a block west to South Water and LaSalle streets. Recognizing the CBOT's growing reputation and upon receiving a charter from the state of Illinois in 1859, the exchange was soon after mandated to set the standards of quality, product uniformity, and routine inspections of grain.[2] Begun as

John Norton's 31-foot painting of Ceres dominates the inside of the CBOT's 12th-floor atrium, which was built in 1982 to connect the original CBOT building with its south annex.

little more than a business club, the CBOT was now setting the standards for the nation's pivotal grain trade and serving an instrumental role for both buyers and sellers.

Outside of its initial formation in 1848, the CBOT's most noteworthy move among its early years occurred in 1865, the year Lee surrendered to Grant at Appomatox to end the Civil War, when the exchange celebrated its new home on the corner of LaSalle and Washington streets. Of its opening, the *Chicago Daily Tribune* reported on August 31, 1865:

The great event so long looked forward to, the great leading topic in Commercial circles of this city, and an interesting one in those of the far off West and East for the past month, has tran-

---

With the commodities exchange industry booming, the Chicago Board of Trade moved into new quarters at LaSalle Street and Jackson Boulevard in 1885.

spired. The new rooms of the Board of Trade of the city of Chicago were opened yesterday with a demonstration mild but imposing, grand in its simplicity, and admirably symbolical in its quietude of the fact that commerce best flourishes in times of peace.[3]

That same year, the CBOT also formalized grain trading and developed the language of "futures contracts," outlining the details of the standardized agreements that would soon become the foundation of the futures industry.

After the celebration of the CBOT's new quarters subsided, the exchange's subsequent years proved a testament to its resilience. After the Great Chicago Fire of 1871 destroyed the six-year-old CBOT building, the exchange constructed temporary quarters on Washington and Market streets to continue its business. When financial panic struck in 1873, the CBOT remained one of the nation's few active and open financial institutions.

Two years later, the CBOT defended itself from a charge by state legislators that it was diverting grain from Chicago by misgrading; such would neither be the first nor last time the CBOT defended itself against criticism. The CBOT also had to deal with the arrival of bucketshops, illegitimate and dishonest copycats of the CBOT model, and the negative perception such operations sparked in public sentiment.

With the growth of futures contracts and increased action in the pits, the CBOT sought another physical move as the industry grew more formalized and speculators entered the fray. On April 29, 1885, the CBOT opened a new building at LaSalle Street and Jackson Boulevard, at the time the city's tallest building and the first commercial structure to use electric lighting. To the gathered group of 4,000 men, CBOT President E. Nelson Blake offered the following words: "For the first time in our history, we are at home, under our root-tree, a wanderer and a tenant no more. ... Soon this hall will resound with the strife of buyer and seller."[4]

As the century turned, the CBOT had transformed the economics of agricultural production and distribution as well as established itself as the nation's premier commodities market, particularly in the grain market. In 1909, the CBOT displayed

its leadership in this regard when it hosted 20 other grain exchanges in a discussion of the industry's current movement as well as its projected future. Years later, as World War I generated market turmoil and wheat prices soared to $3.25 a bushel, the CBOT held steady. Soon after the war's end, the CBOT was setting new records, trading 26.9 billion bushels of wheat in 1925 alone. The next year, 1926, the Board of Trade Clearing Corporation was established to guarantee all CBOT trades, then viewed as an insightful and modern move in an evolving industry.

"That was the first clearing corporation that eliminated counter party risk ... and basically created a tremendous efficiency for the marketplace," said the CBOT's current Chairman Charles P. Carey, whose father was a member from 1948 to 1977. "It eliminated an old-fashioned method for clearing trades counter party to counter party. Then, you had an explosion."[5]

By 1929, with the Great Depression still in its infancy, the exchange moved to a temporary home

Above: During the 1920s, traders gathered on the expansive CBOT trading floor. *(Photo by Kaufmann, Weiner & Fabry Co.)*

Below: In the midst of World War I, the CBOT hosted a contingent of armed services personnel at holiday time.

The CBOT began construction on a new building in 1929. The 45-story structure, completed in 1930, dominated the city skyline.

in Chicago as a new 45-story building was erected on the LaSalle Street and Jackson Boulevard site that housed its present quarters—this as membership seats in the exchange topped $60,000. A year later, traders and staff moved into the new $22 million Board of Trade building, a skyscraper that boasted 16 more stories than Chicago's famed Wrigley Building, at the time the city's tallest structure. Members of the exchange marched from their temporary quarters to their new permanent home at 141 West Jackson Boulevard in a ceremonious and symbolic parade marking the CBOT's new heights as an exchange in both prestige and influence.

Then a dominant presence in the Chicago landscape, the CBOT remains one of Chicago's most revered and recognized structures. In a banquet celebrating the building's dedication on June 9, 1930, CBOT President John A. Bunnell reminded the 2,400 guests of the exchange's vital purpose in the financial arena:

The law of supply and demand is still working and is always bound in the end to the rule. The Chicago Board of Trade and other organized exchanges of the country are carrying on and maintain a year-round steady market for the products of the soil and of man, guaranteeing to everyone fair treatment and honest dealing.[6]

While 1936 witnessed the creation of the CBOT's soybean futures contract, a hallmark product for the exchange, the CBOT endured World War II, price controls, and postwar rebuilding for much of the 1940s. The 1950s, however, were a decade characterized by postwar progress in Chicago and throughout the nation. After surviving the wartime controls of the Second World War, the CBOT began capitalizing on the promise of its soybean futures contract first launched in 1936 as well as that commodity's offspring. In 1950, the CBOT released its soybean oil contract and followed that a year later with soybean meal futures.

In 1956, the CBOT hired Richard C. Liebenow as its president, the first paid nonmember to hold the distinguished post in the exchange's 108-year history. The 34-year-old Liebenow, who became the youngest head of any of the nation's commodity or security exchanges, joined with the CBOT's first elected chairman, Julius Mayer, to comprise the exchange's new leadership team.[7] The move, reported the *Chicago Tribune*, was "a recognition of a modern trend of stepped up public relations, an art in which the 82 founders of the exchange in 1848 were past masters. Their specialties were free lunches every day to attract businessmen into the exchange to examine the atmosphere and perhaps become members." The affable Liebenow, it was reasoned, could devote his full efforts to advancing the exchange by centralizing administrative duties and carrying out policy.[8]

Throughout the 1960s, the CBOT continued its move toward a more modern institution reflecting the growing momentum and demands of the futures industry. Electronic price display boards were installed in 1967, replacing the primitive chalkboards and thereby slashing price-reporting time to seconds. In 1968, the exchange launched a pair of innovative initiatives. First, the CBOT introduced its iced broilers contract, the exchange's first non-grain–related commodity, and soon after followed that with the release of a silver futures contract in 1969. These new landmark products signaled the CBOT's systematic positioning for future growth.

New administrative changes in the final years of the 1960s also demonstrated the CBOT's forward thinking. The CBOT named its first public directors in 1968, a list that included John Hopkins University President Milton S. Eisenhower, former Bureau of the Budget Director Charles L. Schultze, and Inland Steel Chairman Joseph I. Block. The

In a special pilot program, CBOT members traded options on soybean futures on their new agricultural trading floor in the annex.

exchange then admitted its first female member in July 1969 with 26-year-old Carol J. Ovitz of Mitchell, Hutchins & Cox, Inc., joining the once exclusively male institution.

Bullish Innovation

While Leo Melamed and CME brethren were developing the International Monetary Market (IMM), a move that would revolutionize the futures industry, the CBOT played a more calculated hand, particularly as the regulatory Commodity Futures Trading Commission (CFTC) continued sharpening its authority. Once the CBOT witnessed the promise of the IMM, however, it quickly moved into action. Members of the CBOT founded the Chicago Board Options Exchange (CBOE), the world's first stock options exchange. Upon the 1973 opening of the CBOE, the *Chicago Tribune* was effusive in its praise:

The establishment of an option exchange should serve the best interests of the public because it will standardize trading in such esoteric instruments, broaden public exposure to this cheaper but more

sophisticated form of investment, and, most important, provide a secondary market for unexpired options, which does not now exist. That it should be established in Chicago is proof of this city's initiative and growing importance in the financial community.[9]

CME long viewed the CBOT as an institution somewhat deliberate in tradition and slow to pursue creative endeavors. Others argued that the CBOT hesitated in making aggressive moves because it did not have to; the CBOT was an institution of authority and standing, prestige and profit, and, therefore, need not take such bold risks. The formation of the CBOE signaled a break from the CBOT's traditionally conservative process, a sign that it, too, was looking to the future's vast potential with a more assertive hand. With that in mind, the CBOT began trading the first interest rate futures contract in 1975. The Government National Mortgage Association futures' debut further positioned the CBOT for drastic increases in trading volume. The CBOT followed that introduction with the release of its U.S. Treasury

bond futures contract, one that would quickly become the world's most actively traded contract.

While CME experienced the most extensive growth in its history, the CBOT also benefited from a tremendous upswing in business. Seeking greater opportunity, the CBOT hopped on the back of its burgeoning Treasury bond futures contract and, in 1982, offered the first options contracts for for U.S. Treasury bond futures. The exchange soon followed with a 10-year Treasury note futures contract. By the end of 1986, the CBOT held the title of the world's most active exchange as trading volume topped 100 million and seat prices rose 16 percent. For both Chicago exchanges—the CBOT and CME—the 1980s market was decidedly bullish.

"The gains at the CBOT and Chicago Merc, the nation's two largest futures exchanges, reflect their burgeoning financial futures trading," the *Wall Street Journal* reported. "Volume of the CBOT's bellwether Treasury bond contract and CME's Standard & Poor's 500 stock-index contract, for example, both soared 30 percent from a year earlier, eclipsing declines in many of the agricultural contracts traded at the exchanges."[10]

When Black Monday devastated the market in October 1987, the CBOT endured the blow with an unwavering resilience. Despite the deafening financial crisis that silenced others, the CBOT was

---

In the early 1980s, the burgeoning financial futures markets moved to the renovated 1930 Art Deco trading hall after the agricultural markets vacated the space in favor of a new floor in the annex.

the world's only major exchange to operate without interruption. Much like CME, the CBOT was forced to defend itself from an array of attacks, its critics arguing that the flurried action of the Chicago trading pits actually caused the crash. Eager to dismiss such misguided criticism, CBOT Chairman Karsten Mahlmann, nicknamed "Cash," could only quip: "No one ever complained when the market was headed up."[11]

Planting Seeds for the Future

Much like its Chicago counterpart, the CBOT similarly noticed the potential of electronic trading and jumped on the possibilities of a global exchange. In 1994, the exchange launched Project A, its first attempt at an after-hours electronic trading system. One year later, the CBOT tested Project A's capabilities when it began trading agricultural products on the system during off-exchange hours.

Despite the vast potential of electronic trading, the CBOT refused to abandon its intense open outcry. The exchange's release of the CBOT Dow Jones Industrial Average Index futures and

The CBOT's north building facade portrays a pair of male images, one of a Mesopotamian, an early provider of wheat, and the second of an American Indian, an early cultivator of maize (corn), which represent the foundation of the exchange's long-held agricultural roots.

options on futures contracts in 1997 was heralded in the *Chicago Tribune* as "the biggest futures product in 20 years."[12] That same year, the CBOT also opened a 60,000-square-foot trading floor for financial futures and futures options, as strong a recognition as any that although agricultural products were etched in the CBOT's history, its future resided in the financial arena. This realization was reinforced in 1998 when the CBOT, celebrating its 150th anniversary, allowed open-outcry trading on financial contracts to run simultaneously with the electronic system throughout the trading day.

In the opening years of the 21st century, the CBOT's operational structure underwent a major overhaul. First, the CBOT adopted a new electronic trading platform powered by LIFFE Connect in November 2005. This announcement coincided with the common clearinghouse agreement the CBOT negotiated with CME. The pact, in which CME agreed to provide all clearing services for CBOT products, was perhaps the first indication that the two Chicago exchanges, both among the world's most active, had largely relinquished the designation as rivals and recognized the potential of cooperative ventures. More important, a spirit of teamwork was born, one heightened by the two-decades-old friendship between the CBOT's Charlie Carey and CME's Terry Duffy.

Although the two exchanges were not competitors within key product offerings, the institutions nevertheless claimed a long and sometimes heated Chicago social competition. CME was the underdog to the CBOT's grandiose standing—"pork belly crapshooters," as CME was once famously referred, against the refined dignity of the CBOT's grain trade. The two institutions often clashed in other ways as well. CME claimed a Jewish-based heritage and a more risk-taking approach; the CBOT, its ranks dominated by the city's most influential ethnic

Trading pits throughout the world have replicated the CBOT's raised octagonal platforms, which allow buyer and seller to more easily see one another.

group—the Irish—most frequently elected to hold its cards closer to its chest and long preferred calculated moves rather than pioneering products. CME prided itself on innovative, aggressive steps some considered too risky—trading pork bellies, the creation of the IMM and the Index and Options Market (IOM), CME Globex, and its emergence as a publicly traded company on the New York Stock Exchange (NYSE). The CBOT often seemed content to simply do its job and do it efficiently, serving much the same role as it had for more than a century and seeing little reason to risk 150 years of sturdy history. Over time, however, the CBOT shed its conservative patina and adopted a more assertive presence in the marketplace.

On April 14, 2005, the CBOT joined CME as a demutualized exchange. Now a for-profit, stock-based holding company and a for-profit, membership exchange, the CBOT adopted the mechanism for a more fast-paced company. On October 19, 2005, the NYSE listed Class A common stock of CBOT Holdings, Inc., on its board at a price of $54 per share. By year's end, the CBOT boasted a record-high 674 million contracts traded on its floor and electronic system. Such results were only bolstered in 2006, when the CBOT released its benchmark agricultural products to the electronic platform along with its trading floor business.

As the 21st century continued unfolding, CME and the CBOT realized they were now more alike than different. Rumors began spreading that the two institutions might one day consolidate their efforts. In previous decades, traders from the respective exchanges had tossed the idea back and forth, imagining the possibilities; leaders, too, had daydreamed about the idea. Politics and social divisions, however, frequently shortened such thoughts before they became actionable.

Finally, leaders from this pair of Chicago's most legendary financial institutions announced the once-unthinkable deal to the public. Led by Duffy and Carey, the longtime friends and onetime hog traders, CME and CBOT agreed to join forces, thereby creating the world's most expansive, diverse, and active futures exchange. The agreement, announced on October 17, 2006, sent immediate vibrations throughout the financial world, while the news was received with a standing ovation in the CBOT's agricultural pits. Carey, whose grandfather, Peter B. Carey, and

uncle, Bernard P. Carey, were both CBOT chairmen, recalled:

> I was concerned because there was a lot of tradition here, and this place just had a great history. I know how this has been a family business with multiple generations coming down here to participate in the grain trade ... so I knew there could be an emotional reaction, and I knew there could have been negative reaction as far as people losing their name and losing what they feel is their tradition and their business history, their family history. All those emotions come into play when you take a step like this.[13]

As 2006 drew to a close, CBOT Holdings and CME Holdings filed the necessary paperwork with the U.S. Securities and Exchange Commission on

On October 19, 2005, the CBOT became a publicly traded company on the New York Stock Exchange (NYSE). Celebrating the honor are (left to right): CBOT Director C. C. Odom; CBOT Vice Chairman Robert Corvino; NYSE CEO John A. Thain; former CBOT Chairman Bernard P. Carey, Sr.; CBOT Chairman Charles P. Carey; CBOT President and CEO Bernard Dan; and CBOT Director Mark Cermak.

December 21, setting in motion the once unimaginable merger of the two landmark Chicago institutions. With 2006 volume at the CBOT surpassing 805 million contracts and CME volume topping 1.4 billion contracts valued at $827 trillion, the merger promised to deliver on all of its potential for an unrivaled commodities exchange centered in the heart of Chicago.

The former hog traders who made the merger happen—CME Executive Chairman Terry Duffy (left) and CBOT Chairman Charlie Carey. Once trading colleagues in CME's hog pits, Duffy and Carey spearheaded the merger talks and got the respective institutions on board with the plan. *(Photo by © David R. Barnes)*

CHAPTER TWELVE

CME AND CBOT: MOVING FORWARD TOGETHER

2006–BEYOND

If we didn't innovate, we wouldn't be sitting where we are today. We'd still be trading butter and eggs. I think that's the hallmark of not only CME but also the CBOT. You have to constantly innovate.

—Terry Duffy

SINCE THE 1970s, A UNION BEtween Chicago Mercantile Exchange (CME) and Chicago Board of Trade (CBOT) has fascinated the imaginations of both traders and exchange leaders. The idea, however, never moved far from fantasy—social divisions and political tie-ups, not to mention an entrenched rivalry, characterized by an annual charity boxing event between the exchanges, resisted such thoughts from moving into any serious discussion.

"This is something that had been talked about since the 1970s, so people [had] debated it for 25 to 30 years," acknowledged CBOT Chairman Charles P. Carey, a third-generation trader at the exchange. "There were just too many turf battles, too many interest groups to deal with, so whoever the visionaries were that tried to talk about it, they had a big uphill battle."[1]

Chicagoans say of their weather's volatility, "If you don't like it, stick around five minutes." Perhaps the same truth applied to the union of CME and CBOT—albeit one measured in decades not minutes. Time brought about mending relationships, open communication, and new industry demands requiring fresh thought.

The foundation for a merger between CME and CBOT formed in 2003 when CME agreed to clear the CBOT's trades. The first significant business partnership between the landmark Chicago insti-

tutions, the common clearing agreement sparked future dialogue and injected a more collaborative spirit into the sometimes-tenuous relationship.

"Once we had [the clearing agreement] done, we had multiple conversations just about life in general, business in general, and cooperating and working together in a very collegial and professional way," said CME Executive Chairman Terry Duffy, CME point man in the common clearing agreement.[2]

Timing Is Everything

By mid-2006, the advancement of the futures industry combined with the public status of Chicago's respective exchanges produced a near-perfect climate for the merger talks to germinate. But before those conversations began, each exchange took bold steps to secure its future mobility and define its position in the marketplace.

For CME, an increased focus on electronic trading, once viewed as the frightful nemesis to a

---

On October 17, 2006, CME and CBOT presented their proposed merger plan to investors. Bantered about for years, the merger combined two of the world's most active futures exchanges into an industry heavyweight twice the size of the next largest exchange. *(Photo by © David R. Barnes)*

somewhat sacred open-outcry model, coupled with its demutualization and groundbreaking 2002 IPO, provided the ideal boost to foster explosive growth and the necessary capital to deal.

"I don't believe that we would have been able to accomplish what we did on October 17, 2006 (the initial agreement to a merger with the CBOT), if we didn't first do what we did on December 6, 2002 [in taking the company public]. I think we truly unlocked the value of CME. It gave us an opportunity to grow our business and distribute our business throughout the world," said Duffy.[3]

Likewise, the CBOT needed to open its marketplace potential. The public offering of Chicago's oldest exchange in October 2005 afforded the CBOT the same flexibility CME had achieved three years prior and has enjoyed ever since. Inspired by CME's demutualization and evolution into a public company, the CBOT felt confident it, too, could put its forward thinking on display and improve prospects for the future. Alluding to both CBOT's public offering and the merger with CME, Carey commented:

A lot of people thought [the CBOT] was a backward-looking association. They hadn't looked under

The new CME Group: leaders of CME and CBOT posed to recognize the formation of the world's largest futures exchange. They are (from left): CME Managing Director and Chief Financial Officer Jamie Parisi, retired CME Chairman Jack Sandner, CBOT President and CEO Bernard Dan, CME CEO Craig Donohue, CME Executive Chairman Terry Duffy, CBOT Chairman Charles P. Carey, CBOT Director Joe Niciforo, CBOT Director C. C. Odom, CBOT Director Jim Donaldson, CBOT Director Chris Stewart, CME outside counsel Jerry Salzman, CME Chairman Emeritus Leo Melamed, CBOT outside counsel Peter B. Carey, and CBOT Senior Vice President and Chief Financial Officer Glen M. Johnson.
(Photo by © David R. Barnes)

the hood. They didn't know that change was about to take place in a dramatic way. But I certainly tip my hat to [CME] because they led the way.[4]

Duffy saw CBOT's move into the public sphere as a crucial step toward increasing dialogue concerning a merger. As the balance of power shifted from the seat-holders to shareholders, the CBOT's public offering put a price tag on the exchange, thereby eliminating the key financial stumbling block to any merger deal.[5]

"That's another reason why the timing was just right because, obviously, they had an opportunity to let their stock be traded and get the valuation on the company," Duffy said.[6]

Although Duffy and Carey first discussed merely extending the common clearing agreement given its confirmed benefits to end-user clients, the respective exchanges, members, and shareholders, the ultimate prize of a potential merger surfaced as an option with an even more favorable end result. Duffy explained:

Charlie and I had conversations, very loose and general, over the years about how we believed that we could hopefully some day put these two great institutions together. But a lot of the pieces of the puzzle had to be put in place.

I had talked to Charlie about extending the clearing agreement because of the huge benefits it was deriving. ... Instead of pursuing that, [we decided that] we should really pursue doing the full transaction instead of trying to pursue conversations that would be lengthy in trying to renegotiate or extend the common clearing link. So that was really what our focus became.[7]

Like Duffy, Carey, too, saw a more appealing and sensible opportunity form before his eyes. "Let's look at the whole enchilada, all the pieces," said Carey. "That was a tune somebody else used to grind, and I kind of borrowed it and said [to Terry Duffy], 'Hey, let's look at the big picture here.'"[8]

Other factors, namely mounting overseas competition, the over-the-counter derivatives market, and the growth of electronic trading, further convinced Duffy and Carey that the time was right to pursue serious merger discussions. Moreover, the decades-old friendship of the two chairmen, along with the regard each person earned at his respective exchange, signaled an opportune time to place old

rivalries aside in the pursuit of smart business. Duffy noted:

I really believe that the climate was just appropriate at the time that we did it and because of the relationship I had built with Charlie over a period of 23 years ... that was instrumental in moving this thing forward.[9]

Prior to going to the boardroom with the plan, Carey and Duffy met independently on numerous occasions to gauge the deal's potential to pass Board approval. Both voiced concern that the shrewdness of the plan would be overshadowed, as it had many times in the past, by the long-held rivalry. After discussing the potential hurdles in their own meetings, the chairmen brought the idea to the respective boards and sought support to move forward in earnest.

"In those Board meetings, I can only speak for myself at CME. There were obviously some comments made ... because of the folklore rivalries that are out there," said Duffy. "But I think every-

On the day of the merger announcement, CME Chairman Emeritus Leo Melamed (left) shared a word with CBOT Chairman Charlie Carey in the hallway of the Chicago Hilton and Towers. *(Photo by © David R. Barnes)*

Above: Less than one year after taking the CBOT public, the two CBOT leaders, CEO Bernard Dan (left) and Chairman Charlie Carey, were sharing even bigger industry news with the announcement of the CBOT merger with CME. Dan was appointed president and CEO of the exchange in November 2002 while Carey earned his first term as chairman in 2003.

Below: CME Chairman Terry Duffy (left) and CEO Craig Donohue brokered the deal that combined CME and CBOT, two landmark Chicago institutions. Under the leadership of Duffy and Donohue, CME established itself as the world's most active futures market. *(Photos by © David R. Barnes)*

body understood that these organizations were completely different than they were as little as two, five, 10, or 20 years ago. They were professionally run, and we were going to do what was in the best interests of our respective shareholders and members. So, yes, [the old rivalry] was brought up, but quickly dismissed."[10]

The same held true with Carey at the CBOT. After collecting his own Board's approval to move ahead with discussions, Carey offered the most direct and targeted words he could on the plan's sensibility:

I think it fits like a glove.[11]

Eventually, the business sense Duffy and Carey championed from the outset captured the minds of the Board members as well. "As you look at the history of these two places, in the early days, it was forming a marketplace and creating trading pits and then adding technology," said Carey. "These places do have a history of innovation, and combined, we'll have no less motivation to innovate, because if we want to stay competitive, you have to innovate."[12]

A Deal for the Futures

On Tuesday, October 17, 2006, nearly 19 years to the day of the 1987 stock market crash and "Black Monday," CME and CBOT leaders gathered at the legendary Chicago Hilton and Towers for an announcement. After three days of around-the-clock negotiations, a deal had been reached—Chicago Mercantile Exchange and Chicago Board of Trade were joining forces. CME agreed to buy the CBOT for $8 billion in stock and a 69 percent ownership in the newly created CME Group Inc. The deal valued the CBOT at $155.26 a share, a significant jump from its $54 public offering price tag just one year prior.

"We believe that with this transaction of becoming the Chicago CME Group, we will be the premier risk-management exchange in the world, based right here in the city of Chicago," Duffy said.[13]

The $8 billion deal, far and away the largest such deal in the growing consolidation of the financial exchange industry, would create an industry Goliath worth some $26 billion in which nine million contracts would pass hands daily at

an annual notional value of $4.2 trillion, a number larger than Germany's annual gross domestic product.[14] At the same time, trading volume in U.S. futures and options experienced an annual growth rate of 25 percent.[15] The combined trading volume of the exchanges would nearly double the output of the next largest exchange, the Frankfurt-based Eurex. With the merger, CME and the CBOT would produce a financial heavyweight capable of battling all competitive challenges and boasting the capital to pursue innovation like never before.

Chairman Emeritus Leo Melamed astutely observed about the merger:

It represents the culmination of a Don Quixote impossible dream. An idea that was born in the 1970s with the launch of financial futures at CME and then at the CBOT. An ambition forged when our two exchanges ushered in the modern era of derivatives. A vision that ignited financial innovation within the American financial service sector and made it first in the world.

It represents a goal that some of us harbored for the past three decades, logical and compelling. One that required time. Time for our ideas to be embraced the world over. Time for our institutions to mature and become public. Time for our cultural heritage to harmonize around the electronic archi-

Chicago's top exchange leaders (left to right): CME CEO Craig Donohue, CBOT Chairman Charlie Carey, CME Chairman Terry Duffy, and CBOT CEO Bernard Dan. Under the terms of the merger, Duffy would become chairman of the combined organization; Carey would serve as vice chairman; Donohue would become CEO; and Dan would remain in his present position overseeing CBOT's products, activities, and customers before moving to an advisory role for the combined organization. *(Photo by © David R. Barnes)*

tecture of today's information technology. And above all, it required a coalition of skilled leaders, beginning with the chairmen of both exchanges who had the good sense and fortitude to make it happen. We have today fulfilled a destiny that will preserve Chicago as the global capital of risk management.[16]

As news of the merger spread, former CME Chairman Jack Sandner said:

What did they used to call Chicago? "The hog butcher of the world." We are now the risk managers of the world.[17]

Upon the merger announcement, stock prices for each exchange surged, CME to a record close

With the CME–CBOT merger, CME relinquished its trading space on Wacker Drive and moved into the CBOT's iconic structure at the foot of LaSalle Street. A staple of the urban landscape since 1930, the CBOT building is among Chicago's most identifiable and architecturally cherished civic structures.

of $516.50 and the CBOT to its own record close of $151.99, a 13 percent jump.[18] Despite that positive news from the market, leaders said rising stock prices would not alter the company's objectives, goals, and innovative spirit. Duffy said:

> *Stock prices go up and down, and we can't manage the business on price. We have to manage the business, and the price will follow—that's really been our mantra here at CME.*
>
> *Even though we have a wide, broad array of products today, benchmark products, we don't know—no one knows—what the world is going to want tomorrow or need tomorrow. So it's still our job, and we will continue to feel it's our job, to find new products [and] what the world is going to need to manage their risk tomorrow. We will continue to innovate new products, and that's something we know is the lifeblood of the future of the exchange.[19]*

Coming Together

Immediately following the announcement, each exchange formed transaction committees to make the merger, estimated to boost profit margins by 37 percent, a seamless one.[20] Representatives who served on the CME transaction committee included: Terry Duffy, Craig Donohue, Phupinder Gill, Leo Melamed, and Jack Sandner. CBOT committee members included Charlie Carey, Bernard Dan, Joseph Niciforo, Christopher Stewart, and C. C. Odom, II.

"There is a need for integration and the fact that you do have two different organizations and two very different ways of doing things, perhaps," said Carey. "We need to smooth those out and make sure there are no issues."[21] Duffy placed equal importance on a competent merger process: "We understand that execution needs to be flawless on this type of transaction," he said.[22]

CME believed it landed upon a formula for success: research, persistence, and prudence leading to an effective outcome—similar to some of its past efforts. A 29-member Board of Directors, to which the CBOT designated nine members, was created to ensure that the merger of the two institutions would be a thorough one benefiting both exchanges. The fact that both exchanges were located in Chicago, had a working knowledge of one another, knew the futures business from the inside out, and traded complementary products, would only help the merger run effectively.

John Davidson, CME's managing director and chief corporate development officer, commented on the strategy utilized to combine these two distinct institutions into a single entity. "The keys to success are detailed planning, which we have already kicked off; a streamlined, highly effective decision-making process; and an eagle-eyed focus on execution," Davidson disclosed in October 2006.[23]

The agreement called for CME Globex, which accounted for more than one billion trades in 2006 alone, to function as CME Group's electronic trading platform for both CME and CBOT products, something Duffy named as an advantage for all traders.

"You'll be on a single platform, and we believe that will enhance the trade because now, you'll have the ability to access all of the Merc's suite of products and the CBOT's suite of products all on one platform. We do believe that will be an enhancement to the end-user," he said.[24]

Meanwhile, the trading pits and administrative offices were slated to move to the CBOT-owned LaSalle Street facilities, an art deco landmark anchored in Chicago's financial district, while administrative headquarters would remain at CME's Wacker Drive headquarters. The move, which positioned the new CME Group and the NYSE as the lone active major exchange trading floors, would end CME's occupation of its Wacker Drive trading floors along the Chicago River in what Duffy said served as the most practical arrangement.[25] "We're not giving up anything by moving our open-outcry facilities to the CBOT's floor [because] the CBOT has put a lot more enhancements to their actual trading facility over the last seven to 10 years than CME," said Duffy of the decision to move floor trading to LaSalle Street.[26]

Although floor traders have long feared an end to their way of life, exchange leaders sought to quiet the concern amid the announcement's frenzy. Open outcry would remain, although trading access would be limited to the members of the exchange presently trading them.[27]

"They've always been looking over their shoulder [in the pits]," said Carey, "and we've managed to transition and grow the marketplace through the side-by-side strategy—and both the Merc and the Chicago Board of Trade employ it. Contrary to our European counterparts, it's been a very successful model for us here at these U.S. exchanges."[28]

Additionally, exchange leaders said the merger would provide an annual savings of $125 million resulting from both technological and trading floor efficiencies as well as administrative costs. Specifically, Carey mentioned CME Globex as the key to a more efficient corporation.

"All these things allow firms to basically become more efficient and to save money and to eliminate duplication," he said. "So the fact that [Globex] is scalable and the fact that [CME] has been constantly able to engineer Globex to meet the needs of their clients is something that we're looking forward to, because now, on one platform, you're going to be able to access this entire suite of products."[29]

The proposed CME–CBOT merger proved a groundbreaking effort that addressed other industry concerns. As customers called for consolidation and the efficiencies that arise from such unions, CME Group positioned itself to answer consumer demands.

"The marketplace is going to require scale. It's going to require efficiency," said Carey. "You're going to have to be global in nature. I think consolidation, the waves of consolidation have started,

---

In 1997, the CBOT opened its financial trading floor in the east building of its sprawling LaSalle Street complex. At 60,000 square feet, the trading floor is not only big enough to store a 747 airplane, but stands as the world's largest physical trading floor. Following the merger's completion, the CBOT's floors host the traders from both Chicago institutions.

and I think that we're going to continue to see consolidation because the market user is going to require the efficiencies and the scale that come out of dealing with one exchange, not five exchanges."[30]

While some analysts feared that the merger would reduce the competition and raise fees, leaders from both CME and CBOT countered that customers would reap the benefits and efficiencies of one electronic trading platform, one open-outcry trading facility, and a single clearinghouse. The market and its participants would be the ultimate beneficiaries of the combined institutions.

"We believe we're going to save $125 million annually in the synergy savings with this transaction," Duffy said. "We also believe that our member-user clients and users will save an additional $70 million a year, which is a big benefit to them."[31]

Indeed, exchange leaders noted extensive evidence suggesting that the new CME Group would be a success as profits poured in and the social divisions that so long hampered business relationships faded. As the *Wall Street Journal* pointed out just days after the merger announcement, CME has never listened to the prognosticators spelling their doom.

"The triumph of the Merc is the story of capitalist adaptation," recorded the *Wall Street Journal.* "It was innovate or die. They picked innovation."[32]

CME survived with a contract on, of all things, pork bellies; it spun a little idea on trading currency into a global financial revolution; and in the early years of the 21st century, while facing intense global competition and the demise of the open-outcry pits, it reinvented the business as a public company and leading technological exchange. With its latest achievement, the purchase of the CBOT and creation of CME Group, Chicago Mercantile Exchange not only secured Chicago's reputation as among the world's most important financial centers but also positioned itself as a growth engine for years to come.

And somewhere amid the noise of the pits, the flurry of CME Globex action, and the critics' voices, the words of former CME President Everette B. Harris were echoing once again: "We didn't know it couldn't be done."

On the Way to Marriage

It was difficult to deny the growing enthusiasm for CME and CBOT's merger announcement. Floor traders spoke of promise and potential. Exchange leaders, meanwhile, cautioned such excitement with the realities of business—the proposed merger remained just that: a proposal. The merger was far from finished, as it needed to achieve both regulatory approval and shareholder endorsement. On December 21, 2006, CME Group took its first step toward finalizing the deal when it filed its registration statement with the Securities and Exchange Commission (SEC), seeking the government's approval. Despite these formidable obstacles, optimism remained high on both Wacker Drive and LaSalle Street.

Yet, a disarming challenge occurred on the way to a seemingly seamless partnership: another suitor entered the fray and attempted to woo the CBOT away from CME. The Atlanta-based Intercontinental Exchange (ICE), a seven-year-old energy futures exchange fresh off a purchase of the New York Board of Trade, contacted the CBOT in March and proposed a merger plan of its own. The CBOT voted to hear ICE's overtures. ICE, an all-electronic exchange, offered a package of cash and stock valued at more than $11 billion, a notable increase over CME's $8 billion pledge. Suddenly, the CBOT had a pair of suitors and a potential bidding war.

Immediately, CME leaders plunged into action. Terry Duffy and Craig Donohue drafted a letter to all CBOT shareholders touting the benefits of a CME–CBOT merger and explaining why CME's offer was superior to any partnership with ICE. Calling ICE's estimated synergies exaggerated, pointing out the integration and execution risks, and noting the CBOT's greater potential in tandem with CME, Duffy and Donohue presented their case for a CME–CBOT union:

> *ICE offers no compelling strategic benefits that enhance CBOT's future growth potential and value creation opportunities. ... ICE is a much smaller player with more limited opportunities for organic growth, a less extensive global presence, a niche customer base, and a more limited track record of innovation.*
>
> *In stark contrast, CME, like CBOT, is a leading global financial institution. Together, CME and CBOT would have a broad and diverse product line, integrated and seamless technologies, a strong platform for innovation, and an experienced management*

team that has worked in the industry for decades. As a united entity, we would solidify Chicago as the home of derivatives trading and ensure that our two exchanges continue to build on our heritages.[33]

CME received an additional endorsement when the U.S. Department of Justice granted regulatory approval for the CME–CBOT merger without conditions on June 11, 2007.

"We have maintained since our merger agreement last October that the Department of Justice would approve our merger," said Donohue following the announcement. "Moving forward with this transaction will allow us to provide increased efficiencies, new trading opportunities, industry-leading trading and clearing platforms, and a combined track record of significant product innovation to our customers worldwide."[34]

Despite confidence that CME and CBOT would eventually stand as partners, CME leaders decided to leave nothing to chance. In preparation for a CBOT shareholders' meeting on July 9, 2007, the CME Board presented its CBOT counterparts a "best and final" offer. CME sweetened its deal to $11.2 billion, an augmented offer aimed at cinching the arrangement. In response, Caledonia Investments, the CBOT's largest shareholder, pledged to fully support the CME offer and the new CME Group.

On July 9, CBOT and CME shareholders gathered at separate locations to vote on the proposed merger, the final step toward a full union. With CME shareholders overwhelmingly approv-

(From left to right): Former Chairman Jack Sandner, Chairman Emeritus Leo Melamed, CME Group Executive Chairman Terry Duffy, CEO Craig Donohue, and Vice Chairman Charlie Carey rang in day one of CME Group. As one company, CME Group is the world's largest and most diverse exchange.

ing the merger, the votes of CBOT shareholders remained the foremost mystery. By the time CBOT votes were counted in mid-week, 87 percent of shareholders approved the CME deal. On Thursday, July 12, the CBOT stock closed a final time at $227.50 and CME Group moved from proposition into reality. An industry behemoth was born, worth some $30 billion and trading upward of 10 million contracts daily in more than 80 countries. Duffy proclaimed:

This is a historic day for both companies, as our two Chicago institutions join to create CME Group. We are grateful for the strong support demonstrated by CME and CBOT shareholders and are confident today's close of our landmark merger will bring substantial benefits to all of our shareholders, customers, members, and the city of Chicago.[35]

CME Group, with legacies in butter and eggs, grain, and pork bellies, could now call itself the world's most diverse and active commodities exchange and envision a future brimming with promise and innovation.

NOTES TO SOURCES

Chapter One

1. *Encyclopedia of Chicago*, (Chicago: University of Chicago Press, 2004), page 9.
2. *An Introduction to Futures and Options* (Chicago: Chicago Mercantile Exchange Education Department, 2004), page 3.
3. Bob Tamarkin, *The Merc* (New York: HarperCollins, 1993), page 9.
4. World Book Online Reference Center, "Commodity Exchange," http://www.worldbookonline.com/.
5. Tamarkin, *The Merc*, 25.
6. World Book Online Reference Center, "Commodity Exchange," http://www.worldbookonline.com/.
7. Tamarkin, *The Merc*, 23.
8. *Encyclopedia of Chicago*, 9.
9. Tamarkin, *The Merc*, 16–17.
10. Ibid., 30.
11. Ibid., 27.
12. Ibid.
13. Ibid., 28.
14. Ibid., 29.
15. Ibid.
16. Ibid., 30.
17. Ibid., 14.
18. Ibid., 33.

Chapter One Sidebar: Forward versus Futures

1. *An Introduction to Futures and Options* (Chicago: Chicago Mercantile Exchange Education Department, 2004), page 5.
2. Ibid., 7.

Chapter One Sidebar: The History of Commodities Markets

1. Wikipedia, "Commodity Markets," http://en.wikipedia.org/.
2. Ibid.
3. Ibid.
4. World Book Online Reference Center, "Osaka," http://www.worldbookonline.com/.
5. Wikipedia, "Commodity Markets," http://en.wikipedia.org/.
6. Ibid.
7. EH.Net Encyclopedia, "A History of Futures Trading in the United States," http://www.eh.net/.
8. *An Introduction to Futures and Options* (Chicago: Chicago Mercantile Exchange Education Department, 2004), page 5.
9. EH.Net Encyclopedia, "A History of Futures Trading in the United States," http://www.eh.net/.

Chapter One Sidebar: The Sherman Antitrust Act

1. World Book Online Reference Center, "Antitrust laws," http://www.worldbookonline.com/.
2. Bob Tamarkin, *The Merc* (New York: HarperCollins, 1993), page 21.
3. Ibid.

Chapter Two

1. Display advertisement No. 1; *Chicago Daily Tribune*, 21 October 1914, page 2.
2. Bob Tamarkin, *The Merc* (New York: HarperCollins, 1993), pages 34–35.
3. Ibid., 35.
4. Ibid., 36.
5. Ibid.
6. Ibid., 38.
7. Ibid., 41.

8. Ibid.
9. Ibid., 41–42.
10. Ibid., 42.
11. Ibid., 44.
12. Ibid., 43.
13. Ibid., 47–48.
14. Ibid., 50.
15. Ibid., 51.
16. Ibid., 56.
17. Ibid., 57.
18. Ibid.
19. Ibid., 65.
20. Ibid.
21. Ibid., 67.
22. Ibid., 75.
23. Ibid., 76.
24. Ibid., 88.
25. Ibid., 90.
26. Ibid., 92.
27. Ibid.
28. Ibid., 92–93.
29. Ibid., 95.

Chapter Two Sidebar:
How It Looks from the Door

1. Bob Tamarkin, *The Merc* (New York: HarperCollins, 1993), page 52.

Chapter Two Sidebar:
Leo Melamed Joins CME

1. Leo Melamed, *Escape to the Futures* (New York: John Wiley & Sons, 1996), page 88.
2. Ibid.
3. Leo Melamed, interview by Jeffrey L. Rodengen, digital recording, 1 November 2005, Write Stuff Enterprises, Inc.

Chapter Three

1. Bob Tamarkin, *The Merc* (New York: HarperCollins, 1993), page 95.
2. Ibid., 101.
3. Ibid., 105.
4. Ibid.
5. Ibid., 111.
6. Ibid., 114.
7. Ibid., 115.
8. Ibid., 117.
9. Ibid., 128.
10. Ibid.
11. Ibid., 130.
12. Ibid., 130–31.
13. Ibid., 132.
14. Ibid., 134–35.
15. Leo Melamed, interview by Jeffrey L. Rodengen, digital recording, 1 November 2005, Write Stuff Enterprises, Inc.
16. Tamarkin, *The Merc*, 137.
17. Ibid., 126.
18. Ibid., 127.

Chapter Four

1. Bob Tamarkin, *The Merc* (New York: HarperCollins, 1993), page 145.
2. Ibid., 146.
3. Leo Melamed, *Escape to the Futures* (New York: John Wiley & Sons, 1996), page 125.
4. Tamarkin, *The Merc*, 145–46.
5. Ibid., 147.
6. Ibid., 150.
7. Melamed, *Escape to the Futures*, 136.
8. Ibid.

9. Tamarkin, *The Merc*, 152.
10. Ibid., 153.
11. Ibid., 160.
12. Ibid., 161.
13. Ibid., 175.
14. Ibid., 147.
15. Ibid., 175.
16. Melamed, *Escape to the Futures*, 143.
17. Tamarkin, *The Merc*, 175.
18. Bob Tamarkin, *The New Gatsbys: Fortunes and Misfortunes of Commodity Traders* (New York: Quill, 1985), page 75.
19. Melamed, *Escape to the Futures*, 171.
20. Ibid., 173.
21. Tamarkin, *The New Gatsbys*, 76–77.
22. Melamed, *Escape to the Futures*, 170.
23. Tamarkin, *The Merc*, 7.
24. Leo Melamed, interview by Jeffrey L. Rodengen, digital recording, 1 November 2005, Write Stuff Enterprises, Inc.
25. Tamarkin, *The Merc*, 180.
26. Tamarkin, *The New Gatsbys*, 77.
27. Milton Friedman, interview by Jeffrey L. Rodengen, digital recording, 14 March 2006, Write Stuff Enterprises, Inc.
28. Tamarkin, *The Merc*, 189.
29. Ibid., 190.
30. Robert Abboud, interview by Jeffrey L. Rodengen, digital recording, 14 March 2006, Write Stuff Enterprises, Inc.

31. Henry Jarecki, interview by Jeffrey L. Rodengen, digital recording, 22 March 2006, Write Stuff Enterprises, Inc.
32. Ibid., 97.
33. Melamed, interview.
34. Tamarkin, *The Merc*, 191.
35. Melamed, interview.
36. Abboud, interview.
37. Tamarkin, *The Merc*, 197.
38. Tamarkin, *The New Gatsbys*, 79.
39. John F. Sandner, "IMM 10th Anniversary Speech," Chicago, 4 June 1982.
40. Tamarkin, *The Merc*, 202.
41. Mitch Fulsher, interview by Jeffrey L. Rodengen, digital recording, 22 March 2006, Write Stuff Enterprises, Inc.
42. Ibid., 201.
43. Thomas Russo, interview by Jeffrey L. Rodengen, digital recording, 10 April 2006, Write Stuff Enterprises, Inc.
44. Bill Shepard, interview by Jeffrey L. Rodengen, digital recording, 2 November 2005, Write Stuff Enterprises, Inc.
45. Tamarkin, *The New Gatsbys*, 92.
46. Melamed, interview.
47. Friedman, interview.

**Chapter Four Sidebar:
Cohen's Bold Advertising**

1. Bob Tamarkin, *The Merc* (New York: HarperCollins, 1993), page 148.
2. Tamarkin, *The Merc*, 149.

**Chapter Four Sidebar:
Milton Friedman Remembered**

1. Bob Tamarkin, *The Merc* (New York: HarperCollins, 1993), page 55.
2. Ibid., 156.
3. Leo Melamed, interview by Jeffrey L. Rodengen, digital recording, 1 November 2005, Write Stuff Enterprises, Inc.

**Chapter Four Sidebar:
Women and CME**

1. Bob Tamarkin, *The Merc* (New York: HarperCollins, 1993), page 154.
2. Ibid.

Chapter Five

1. Leo Melamed, *Escape to the Futures* (New York: John Wiley & Sons, 1996), page 160.
2. Ibid.
3. Edward Lee, "CME's New Home Sees First Trade Day," *Chicago Tribune*, 28 November 1972.
4. Edward Lee, "'New' Commodity, Too-POT," *Chicago Tribune*, 21 November 1972.
5. Edward Lee, "CME's New Home Sees First Trade Day," *Chicago Tribune*, 28 November 1972.
6. Melamed, *Escape to the Futures*, 199.
7. Ibid., 198.

8. Ibid., 199.
9. Ibid., 209.
10. Bob Tamarkin, *The Merc* (New York: HarperCollins, 1993), page 220.
11. Robert Abboud, interview by Jeffrey L. Rodengen, digital recording, 14 March 2006, Write Stuff Enterprises, Inc.
12. Melamed, *Escape to the Futures*, 210.
13. Tamarkin, *The Merc*, 221.
14. Clayton Yeutter, interview by Jeffrey L. Rodengen, digital recording, 27 March 2006, Write Stuff Enterprises, Inc.
15. Beverly Splane, interview by Jeffrey L. Rodengen, digital recording, 17 March 2006, Write Stuff Enterprises, Inc.
16. Melamed, *Escape to the Futures*, 222.
17. Ibid., 242.
18. Tamarkin, *The Merc*, 236.
19. Leo Melamed, interview by Jeffrey L. Rodengen, digital recording, 1 November 2005, Write Stuff Enterprises, Inc.
20. Bill Shepard, interview by Jeffrey L. Rodengen, digital recording, 2 November 2005, Write Stuff Enterprises, Inc.
21. Melamed, *Escape to the Futures*, 247.
22. Ibid., 248.
23. Tamarkin, *The Merc*, 237.
24. Melamed, *Escape to the Futures*, 245.

25. Ibid., 161.
26. Ibid.
27. Ibid., 161–62.
28. Tamarkin, *The Merc*, 226.
29. Melamed, *Escape to the Futures*, 238.
30. Tamarkin, *The Merc*, 226–227.
31. "T-bill Futures Trade Starts with Flourish," *Chicago Tribune*, 7 January 1976.
32. Melamed, *Escape to the Futures*, 229.
33. Tamarkin, *The Merc*, 239.
34. Melamed, *Escape to the Futures*, 229.
35. Ibid.
36. Ibid., 262.
37. Tamarkin, *The Merc*, 225.
38. Yeutter, interview.
39. Melamed, *Escape to the Futures*, 263.
40. Ibid., 269–70.
41. Ibid., 273–74.
42. Dan Glickman, interview by Jeffrey L. Rodengen, digital recording, 17 March 2006, Write Stuff Enterprises, Inc.
43. Melamed, *Escape to the Futures*, 276.
44. Ibid., 266.
45. Tamarkin, *The Merc*, 243.
46. Yeutter, interview.
47. Tamarkin, *The Merc*, 259.
48. Ibid., 260.

Chapter Five Sidebar: Jack Sandner's Rise

1. Bob Tamarkin, *The New Gatsbys: Fortunes and Misfortunes of Commodity Traders* (New York: Quill, 1985), pages 185–87.
2. Ibid., 187–88.
3. Ibid., 190.
4. Ibid., 191.

Chapter Five Sidebar: The Free Market Spirit in Action

1. Bob Tamarkin, *The Merc* (New York: HarperCollins, 1993), page 253.
2. Ibid., 248.

Chapter Six

1. Bob Tamarkin, *The Merc* (New York: HarperCollins, 1993), page 261.
2. Ibid., 266–67.
3. Leo Melamed, interview by Jeffrey L. Rodengen, digital recording, 1 November 2005, Write Stuff Enterprises, Inc.
4. Ibid.
5. Tamarkin, *The Merc*, 270.
6. Melamed, interview.
7. Ibid.
8. Tamarkin, *The Merc*, 270.
9. Ibid., 271.
10. Ibid.
11. Leo Melamed, *Escape to the Futures* (New York: John Wiley & Sons, 1996), page 291.
12. Ibid., 300.
13. Jack Sandner, interview by Jeffrey L. Rodengen, digital recording, 10 March 2006, Write Stuff Enterprises, Inc.
14. Leo Melamed, "A History of the IMM" (unpublished), 1982.
15. Melamed, *Escape to the Futures*, 298.
16. Ibid.
17. Jack Sandner, interview by Jeffrey L. Rodengen, digital recording, 17 February 2006, Write Stuff Enterprises, Inc.
18. Leo Melamed, interview by Jeffrey L. Rodengen, digital recording, 7 February 2006, Write Stuff Enterprises, Inc.
19. Tamarkin, *The Merc*, 273.
20. Ibid., 266.
21. Melamed, *Escape to the Futures*, 303.
22. Tamarkin, *The Merc*, 268.
23. Clayton Yeutter, interview by Jeffrey L. Rodengen, digital recording, 27 March 2006, Write Stuff Enterprises, Inc.
24. Melamed, *Escape to the Futures*, 304.
25. Tamarkin, *The Merc*, 288.
26. Ibid., 290.
27. Melamed, *Escape to the Futures*, 315.
28. Ibid., 316.
29. Ibid., 319.
30. Ibid., 320.
31. Beverly Splane, interview by Jeffrey L. Rodengen, digital recording, 17 March 2006, Write Stuff Enterprises, Inc.
32. Tamarkin, *The Merc*, 313.
33. Melamed, *Escape to the Futures*, 320.

Chapter Six Sidebar:
The IMM's 10ᵗʰ Anniversary

1. Leo Melamed, Address to Members, 4 June 1982.

Chapter Six Sidebar:
S&P 500 Index Soars

1. Jack Sandner, Address to Members, 1982.

Chapter Six Sidebar:
Terry Duffy Enters the Pits

1. Terry Duffy, interview by Jeffrey L. Rodengen, digital recording, 2 November 2005, Write Stuff Enterprises, Inc.

Chapter Six Sidebar:
Brodsky Joins CME

1. Laurie Cohen, "Brodsky Steering Merc into Securities Market," *Chicago Tribune*, 20 October 1982, C9.
2. Leo Melamed, *Escape to the Futures* (New York: John Wiley & Sons, 1996), pages 313–34.
3. Bob Tamarkin, *The Merc* (New York: HarperCollins, 1993), page 283.
4. Ibid., 285.
5. Melamed, *Escape to the Futures*, 325.
6. William J. Brodsky, interview by Jeffrey L. Rodengen, digital recording, 31 March 2006, Write Stuff Enterprises, Inc.

Chapter Seven

1. Ian Verchere, "Chicago: Knee Deep in Liquidity," *Euromoney*, October 1986.
2. Bob Tamarkin, *The Merc* (New York: HarperCollins, 1993), page 307.
3. Ibid.
4. Jack Sandner, Address to CME Membership, 2 January 1987.
5. Leo Melamed, *Escape to the Futures* (New York: John Wiley & Sons, 1996), page 325.
6. Sandner, Address to CME Membership.
7. Melamed, *Escape to the Futures*, 340.
8. Tamarkin, *The Merc*, 317.
9. Ibid., 318.
10. Ibid., 316.
11. Melamed, *Escape to the Futures*, 331.
12. Tamarkin, *The Merc*, 319.
13. Ibid., 320.
14. William J. Brodsky, interview by Jeffrey L. Rodengen, digital recording, 31 March 2006, Write Stuff Enterprises, Inc.
15. Leo Melamed, "Responding to Globalization: A CME Perspective" (unpublished), 1987.
16. Melamed, *Escape to the Futures*, 332.
17. Leo Melamed, "Responding to Globalization: An Exchange Perspective," Barron's Special Edition on Global Markets, 28 September 1987.

18. Tamarkin, *The Merc*, 379.
19. Ibid., 379–80.
20. Melamed, "Responding to Globalization," 28 September 1987.
21. Tamarkin, *The Merc*, 380.
22. Terry Duffy, interview by Jeffrey L. Rodengen, digital recording, 16 February 2006, Write Stuff Enterprises, Inc.
23. Craig Donohue, interview by Jeffrey L. Rodengen, digital recording, 17 February 2006, Write Stuff Enterprises, Inc.
24. Tamarkin, *The Merc*, 382.
25. David Gomach, interview by Jeffrey L. Rodengen, digital recording, 10 March 2006, Write Stuff Enterprises, Inc.
26. Myron Scholes, interview by Jeffrey L. Rodengen, digital recording, 5 May 2006, Write Stuff Enterprises, Inc.
27. Tamarkin, *The Merc*, 324.
28. John Davidson, interview by Jeffrey L. Rodengen, digital recording, 7 March 2006, Write Stuff Enterprises, Inc.
29. Tamarkin, *The Merc*, 323.
30. Davidson, interview.
31. Ibid.
32. Brodsky, interview.
33. Barry Lind, interview by Jeffrey L. Rodengen, digital recording, 5 April 2006, Write Stuff Enterprises, Inc.
34. Sandner, Address to CME Membership.
35. Melamed, *Escape to the Futures*, 354.

36. Martin Gepsman, interview by Jeffrey L. Rodengen, digital recording, 18 May 2006, Write Stuff Enterprises, Inc.

37. Tamarkin, *The Merc*, 357.

38. Randy McKay, interview by Jeffrey L. Rodengen, digital recording, 15 March 2006, Write Stuff Enterprises, Inc.

39. Ibid.

40. Melamed, *Escape to the Futures*, 358.

41. Davidson, interview.

42. Melamed, *Escape to the Futures*, 359.

43. Sandner, Address to CME Membership.

44. Melamed, *Escape to the Futures*, 363.

45. Ibid., 366.

46. Davidson, interview.

47. Yra Harris, interview by Jeffrey L. Rodengen, digital recording, 16 February 2006, Write Stuff Enterprises, Inc.

48. Jerry Salzman, interview by Jeffrey L. Rodengen, digital recording, 19 May 2006, Write Stuff Enterprises, Inc.

49. Sandner, Address to CME Membership.

50. Gomach, interview.

51. Tamarkin, *The Merc*, 337.

52. Ibid., 338.

53. Sandner, interview.

54. Tamarkin, *The Merc*, 338–39.

55. House Committee on Agriculture, Nutrition, and Forestry, Oral Testimony of Jack Sandner, Chairman of the Board of Governors Chicago Mercantile Exchange, 27 April 1988.

56. Burton G. Malkiel, "Stressed-Out Stock Markets ..." *New York Times*, 15 June 1990, A29.

57. Tamarkin, *The Merc*, 335.

58. Rick Redding, interview by Jeffrey L. Rodengen, digital recording, 17 February 2006, Write Stuff Enterprises, Inc.

59. Davidson, interview.

60. Todd Petzel, interview by Jeffrey L. Rodengen, digital recording, 17 March 2006, Write Stuff Enterprises, Inc.

61. Duffy, interview.

62. Tamarkin, *The Merc*, 387–88.

63. Ibid., 386.

64. Jack Sandner, Address to CME Membership, 9 January 1989.

Chapter Eight

1. Bob Tamarkin, *The Merc* (New York: HarperCollins, 1993), page 406.

2. William B. Crawford, Jr., "Merc Looks to Keep Futures Leadership: Times Now Are Critical, Chief Says," *Chicago Tribune*, 21 April 1991.

3. Tamarkin, *The Merc*, 414.

4. William B. Crawford, Jr., "Globex Maiden Run Nears 2,000 Trades," *Chicago Tribune*, 27 June 1992.

5. Leo Melamed, *Escape to the Futures* (New York: John Wiley & Sons, 1996), page 424.

6. William B. Crawford, Jr., "The Lords of Trade," *Chicago Tribune* Sunday Magazine, 22 March 1992.

7. Ibid.

8. Ibid.

9. Ibid.

10. Tamarkin, *The Merc*, 414–15.

11. Kurt Eichenwald, "Chicago Merc Plans Largest Trading Floor," *New York Times*, 19 June 1992.

12. Janet Kidd Stewart, "New Floor Helps Merc Move Futures to Next Level, *Chicago Sun-Times*, 15 June 1993.

13. Jack Sandner, interview by Jeffrey L. Rodengen, digital recording, 17 February 2006, Write Stuff Enterprises, Inc.

14. Ibid.

15. "Dow Plummets on News of Rate Hike," *Pantagraph* (Bloomington, Illinois), 5 February 1994.

16. Sandner, interview.

17. Ibid.

18. Ibid.

19. Terry Duffy, interview by Jeffrey L. Rodengen, digital recording, 16 February 2006, Write Stuff Enterprises, Inc.

20. Jim Oliff, interview by Jeffrey L. Rodengen, digital recording, 20 April 2006, Write Stuff Enterprises, Inc.

21. David Roeder, "Dow Jones Futures Debut October 6," *Chicago Sun-Times*, 21 August 1997.

22. Aaron Lucchetti, "CME Is Considering Electronic Orders for Its Mini-S&P Contract," *Wall Street Journal*, 3 July 1997.

23. Sandner, interview.

24. Greg Burns, "A Maximum Debut for 'E-mini' Contract," *Chicago Tribune*, 10 September 1997.

25. Craig Donohue, interview by Jeffrey L. Rodengen, digital recording, 17 February 2006, Write Stuff Enterprises, Inc.

26. Greg Burns, "50,000 Dow Contracts Traded on First Day," *Chicago Tribune*, 7 October 1997.

27. Donohue, interview.

28. Sandner, interview.

29. Chicago Mercantile Exchange, Annual Report, 1997.

30. Rick Kilcollin, interview by Jeffrey L. Rodengen, digital recording, 23 March 2006, Write Stuff Enterprises, Inc.

31. Donohue, interview.

32. Ibid.

33. Ibid.

34. John R. Roberts, interview by Jeffrey L. Rodengen, digital recording, 1 November 2005, Write Stuff Enterprises, Inc.

Chapter Eight Sidebar: CME and the Community

1. Chicago Mercantile Exchange, *Innovation* (Chicago: CME, 2005).

2. CME Center for Innovation Mayoral Award for Student Achievement, Chicago Mercantile Exchange (Chicago: CME, 2006).

3. Ali Fatemi, interview by Jeffrey L. Rodengen, digital recording, 16 February 2006, Write Stuff Enterprises, Inc.

4. Amicus, Chicago Mercantile Exchange (Chicago: CME, 2006).

5. Chicago Mercantile Exchange, 2004 Annual Charitable Report to the Community, disclosure statement, 2005.

Chapter Nine

1. George Gunset, "Investment Banker New Merc President," *Chicago Tribune*, 19 January 2000, page 3.

2. Terry Duffy, interview by Jeffrey L. Rodengen, digital recording, 2 November 2005, Write Stuff Enterprises, Inc.

3. Phupinder Gill, interview by Jeffrey L. Rodengen, digital recording, 16 February 2006, Write Stuff Enterprises, Inc.

4. Jim Oliff, interview by Jeffrey L. Rodengen, digital recording, 20 April 2006, Write Stuff Enterprises, Inc.

5. Bill Miller, interview by Jeffrey L. Rodengen, digital recording, 14 April 2006, Write Stuff Enterprises, Inc.

6. Duffy, interview.

7. Jamie Parisi interview by Jeffrey L. Rodengen, digital recording, 2 November 2005, Write Stuff Enterprises, Inc.

8. David Gomach, interview by Jeffrey L. Rodengen, digital recording, 10 March 2006, Write Stuff Enterprises, Inc.

9. Ibid.

10. Oliff, interview.

11. John McPartland interview by Jeffrey L. Rodengen, digital recording, 2 April 2006, Write Stuff Enterprises, Inc.

12. Duffy, interview.

13. Gomach, interview.

14. John Peschier, interview by Jeffrey L. Rodengen, digital recording, 2 November 2005, Write Stuff Enterprises, Inc.

15. John R. Roberts, interview by Jeffrey L. Rodengen, digital recording, 1 November 2005, Write Stuff Enterprises, Inc.

16. Thomas A. Russo, interview by Jeffrey L. Rodengen, digital recording, 10 April 2006, Write Stuff Enterprises, Inc.

17. Robert Glauber, interview by Jeffrey L. Rodengen, digital recording, 3 April 2006, Write Stuff Enterprises, Inc.

18. Terry Duffy, 2003 Remarks to Shareholders, 23 April 2004.

19. Ibid.

20. "OneChicago: Single-stock Futures Trading Launch Set," *Chicago Tribune*, 25 September 2002, page 2.
21. Gomach, interview.
22. Ibid.
23. Duffy, interview.
24. Donohue, interview.
25. Duffy, interview.
26. Jack Sandner, interview by Jeffrey L. Rodengen, digital recording, 17 February 2006, Write Stuff Enterprises, Inc.
27. Duffy, interview.
28. Gomach, interview.
29. Matt Krantz, "Chicago Mercantile Exchange to Go Public," *USA Today*, 5 December 2002, B3.
30. Duffy, interview.
31. Terry Duffy, 2003 Remarks to Shareholders, 23 April 2004.
32. Carol Norton, interview by Jeffrey L. Rodengen, digital recording, 7 February 2006, Write Stuff Enterprises, Inc.
33. Oliff, interview.
34. Tad Davis, interview by Jeffrey L. Rodengen, digital recording, 12 April 2006, Write Stuff Enterprises, Inc.
35. John Davidson, interview by Jeffrey L. Rodengen, digital recording, 7 March 2006, Write Stuff Enterprises, Inc.
36. Oliff, interview.
37. CME Press Release, "CME Announces Common Clearing Link Is Fully Operational; CME Clearing House Now the Largest in the World," 5 January 2004.
38. Davis, interview.
39. Gill, interview.
40. CME Press Release, "CME Announces Common Clearing Link Is Fully Operational; CME Clearing House Now the Largest in the World," 5 January 2004.
41. Gill, interview.
42. Terry Duffy, 2003 Remarks to Shareholders, 23 April 2004.
43. Duffy, interview.
44. Gomach, interview.
45. CME Press Release, "CME Launches E-mini NASDAQ Composite Index Futures," 27 October 2003.
46. Terry Duffy, 2003 Remarks to Shareholders, 23 April 2004.
47. Duffy, interview.

Chapter Nine Sidebar:
An Evolving Relationship

1. Dan Glickman, interview by Jeffrey L. Rodengen, digital recording, 22 March 2006, Write Stuff Enterprises, Inc.
2. Bob Tamarkin, *The Merc* (New York: HarperCollins, 1993), page 258.
3. Tad Davis, interview by Jeffrey L. Rodengen, digital recording, 12 April 2006, Write Stuff Enterprises, Inc.
4. Susan E. Miller, "CBOT–Merc Deal Debated," *Chicago Tribune*, 15 October 1998, page 52.
5. Yra Harris, interview by Jeffrey L. Rodengen, digital recording, 16 February 2006, Write Stuff Enterprises, Inc.
6. Randy McKay, interview by Jeffrey L. Rodengen, digital recording, 26 March 2006, Write Stuff Enterprises, Inc.
7. Terry Duffy, interview by Jeffrey L. Rodengen, digital recording, 16 February 2006, Write Stuff Enterprises, Inc.
8. Milton Friedman, PhD, interview by Jeffrey L. Rodengen, digital recording, 16 March 2006, Write Stuff Enterprises, Inc.

Chapter Nine Sidebar:
CME's Competitive Markets
Advisory Council

1. Leo Melamed, notes provided to Colleen Lazar, 10 June 2007.

Chapter Ten

1. CME Press Release, "CME to Launch Yen and U.S. Dollar–based Nikkei 225 Index Futures Contracts on Globex," 26 January 2004.
2. CME Press Release, "Chicago Mercantile Exchange Sets February 8 Launch for CPI Futures," 16 January 2004.
3. CME Press Release, "CME's New Globex Learning Center and Visitors Center Opening Gala," 4 March 2004.
4. Ibid.

5. CME Press Release, "Chicago Mercantile Exchange Launches Aggressive New European Pricing Plan," 10 November 2003.

6. CME Press Release, "CME Unveils Incentive Program Targeting New Globex Traders," 28 June 2004.

7. CME Press Release, "Chicago Mercantile, Shanghai Futures Exchanges Sign Agreement," 18 March 2004.

8. CME Press Release, "CME Establishes Competitive Markets Advisory Council," 19 March 2004.

9. CME Press Release, "Chicago Mercantile Exchange and Reuters Join Forces to Offer Futures Trading," 24 May 2004.

10. CME Press Release, "Chicago Mercantile Exchange Extends Trading Hours on Globex," 6 May 2004.

11. Terry Duffy, 2004 Remarks to Shareholders, 21 April 2004.

12. Mark Skertic, "Between the Pits and PCs, Traders Find Middle Ground," *Chicago Tribune*, 10 April 2004.

13. Mark Skertic, "Europeans 'Light Fire' Under CBOT, Merc," *Chicago Tribune*, 25 July 2004.

14. Terry Duffy and Craig Donohue, Letter to the Editor, *Chicago Tribune*, 8 August 2004.

15. Terry Duffy, interview by Christine Romans, "Street Sweep," CNN, 26 October 2004.

16. "Caterpillar Profit Up but Short of Forecast; Merc Jumps," *Chicago Tribune*, 23 July 2004.

17. Terry Duffy, interview by Jeffrey L. Rodengen, digital recording, 16 February 2006, Write Stuff Enterprises, Inc.

18. Terry Duffy, 2005 Remarks to Shareholders, 27 April 2005.

19. Ibid.

20. Leo Melamed, "Innovation," Speech delivered at CME Center for Innovation Inaugural Event, Chicago, 18 June 2003.

21. Leo Melamed, interview by Jeffrey L. Rodengen, digital recording, 7 February 2006, Write Stuff Enterprises, Inc.

22. CME Press Release, "CME, Standard & Poor's Announce Extension of Exclusive License for S&P Index Futures Contract," 23 September 2005.

23. Todd Petzel, interview by Jeffrey L. Rodengen, digital recording, 17 March 2006, Write Stuff Enterprises, Inc.

24. Rich Redding, interview by Jeffrey L. Rodengen, digital recording, 6 February 2006, Write Stuff Enterprises, Inc.

25. Michael Moscow, interview by Jeffrey L. Rodengen, digital recording, 23 March 2006, Write Stuff Enterprises, Inc.

26. Dan Glickman, interview by Jeffrey L. Rodengen, digital recording, 7 March 2006, Write Stuff Enterprises, Inc.

27. Duffy, interview.

28. Bill Miller, interview by Jeffrey L. Rodengen, digital recording, 14 April 2006, Write Stuff Enterprises, Inc.

29. John Peschier, interview by Jeffrey L. Rodengen, digital recording, 2 November 2005, Write Stuff Enterprises, Inc.

30. CME Press Release, "Chicago Mercantile Exchange to Dual List on the NASDAQ Stock Market," 28 April 2005.

31. CME Press Release, "CME–NASDAQ Announce Extension of Exclusivity Agreement for NASDAQ-100 Futures; Will Develop New Products Including First-ever Biotechnology Futures," 28 April 2005.

32. Howard Packowitz, "Merc Stock Reaches Record Price Riding Wave of Uncertainty," *Chicago Sun-Times*, 21 September 2005.

33. Russell Wasendorf, Sr., "2005 Co-Persons of the Year," *SFO*, December 2005.

34. CME Web site, "2005 Facts and Figures," http://www.cme.com/about/ins/caag/FacFigu2803.html/.

35. Wasendorf, Sr., "2005 Co-Persons of the Year."

36. Ibid.

37. Andrew Countryman, "Merc Surges to Record Profit," *Chicago Tribune*, 27 April 2005.

38. Hans Stoll, interview by Jeffrey L. Rodengen, digital recording, 25 April 2006, Write Stuff Enterprises, Inc.

39. Jamie Parisi, interview by Jeffrey L. Rodengen, digital recording, 2 November 2005, Write Stuff Enterprises, Inc.

40. Craig Donohue, interview by Jeffrey L. Rodengen, digital recording, 10 November 2005, Write Stuff Enterprises, Inc.

41. Ibid.

42. Phupinder Gill, interview by Jeffrey L. Rodengen, digital recording, 16 February 2006, Write Stuff Enterprises, Inc.

43. David Prosperi, interview by Jeffrey L. Rodengen, digital recording, 1 November 2005, Write Stuff Enterprises, Inc.

44. Ibid.

45. Jim Krause, interview by Jeffrey L. Rodengen, digital recording, 16 February 2006, Write Stuff Enterprises, Inc.

46. Gill, interview.

47. Prosperi, interview.

48. David Roeder, "When It's Time to Deal, CME Needn't Look Far," *Chicago Sun-Times*, 18 September 2005.

49. "Mergers," *Sun-Sentinel*, 30 June 2005, 3D.

50. "Merc Shares Top $200 on NYSE Rumors," *Chicago Tribune*, 12 November 2004.

51. Robert Abboud, interview by Jeffrey L. Rodengen, digital recording, 14 March 2006, Write Stuff Enterprises, Inc.

52. Parisi, interview.

53. John R. Roberts, interview by Jeffrey L. Rodengen, digital recording, 1 November 2005, Write Stuff Enterprises, Inc.

54. Myron Scholes, interview by Jeffrey L. Rodengen, digital recording, 2 May 2006, Write Stuff Enterprises, Inc.

55. Craig Donohue, interview by Jeffrey L. Rodengen, digital recording, 2 May 2006, Write Stuff Enterprises, Inc.

56. John Peschier, interview by Jeffrey L. Rodengen, digital recording, 2 November 2005, Write Stuff Enterprises, Inc.

57. Rick Redding, interview by Jeffrey L. Rodengen, digital recording, 17 February 2006, Write Stuff Enterprises, Inc.

58. Donohue, interview.

59. Duffy, interview.

60. Michael Moscow, interview by Jeffrey L. Rodengen, digital recording, 3 March 2006, Write Stuff Enterprises, Inc.

**Chapter Ten Sidebar:
Life in the Pits**

1. Jamie Parisi, interview by Jeffrey L. Rodengen, digital recording, 2 November 2005, Write Stuff Enterprises, Inc.

2. Patrick Lynch, interview by Jeffrey L. Rodengen, digital recording, 19 April 2006, Write Stuff Enterprises, Inc.

3. Martin Callaghan, interview by Jeffrey L. Rodengen, digital recording, 28 July 2006, Write Stuff Enterprises, Inc.

4. Bill Shepard, interview by Jeffrey L. Rodengen, digital recording, 2 November 2005, Write Stuff Enterprises, Inc.

5. Barbara Brotman, "Chicago Speak," *Chicago Tribune*, 21 October 1993.

6. Bob Tamarkin, *The New Gatsbys: Fortunes and Misfortunes of Commodity Traders* (New York: Quill, 1985).

7. Randy McKay, interview by Jeffrey L. Rodengen, digital recording, 26 March 2006, Write Stuff Enterprises, Inc.

8. Lynch, interview.
9. CME Press Release, "CME Introduces Options on Futures Trading on Handheld Devices," 22 March 2005.
10. Callaghan, interview.

Chapter Ten Sidebar: Today's CME Leaders

1. Ann Therese Palmer, "Adapting to Merc's Evolving Needs a Key to Chief Executive's Success," *Chicago Tribune*, 27 September 2004.
2. Phupinder Gill, interview by Jeffrey L. Rodengen, digital recording, 16 February 2006, Write Stuff Enterprises, Inc.
3. Jim Oliff, interview by Jeffrey L. Rodengen, digital recording, 20 April 2006, Write Stuff Enterprises, Inc.

Chapter Ten Sidebar: CME Trust

1. Leo Melamed, notes provided to Colleen Lazar, 10 June 2007.

Chapter Ten Sidebar: CME Globex Volume Grows

1. Chicago Mercantile Exchange, Interim Capabilities Brochure, 30 July 2007.

Chapter Eleven

1. Susan Diesenhouse, "Merc Sees Shares Rise on Rumors; Board of Trade Stock Falls; Both Subject of Merger Speculation," *Chicago Tribune*, 10 October 2006.
2. "Chicago Board of Trade: Opening of the New Hall," *Chicago Daily Tribune*, 31 August 1865.
3. Ibid.
4. "Ready for Business," *Chicago Daily Tribune*, 30 April 1885.
5. Charles P. Carey, interview by Jeffrey L. Rodengen, digital recording, 1 March 2007, Write Stuff Enterprises, Inc.
6. "Lash Radicals at Banquet of Board of Trade," *Chicago Daily Tribune*, 10 June 1930.
7. "R. C. Liebenow President of Grain Market," *Chicago Daily Tribune*, 22 August 1956.
8. Russell Freeburg, "Board of Trade Executives," *Chicago Daily Tribune*, 26 August 1956.
9. "A New Exchange," *Chicago Tribune*, 27 April 1973.
10. Michael Siconofi and Jean Marie Brown, "Prices for Commodity Exchange Seats Surge on Booming Volume in Contracts," *Wall Street Journal*, 12 January 1987.
11. Carol Jouzaitis and Michael Arndt, "LaSalle Street Put on the Defensive," *Chicago Tribune*, 26 October 1987.
12. David Roeder, "Dow futures and Options Start Trade," *Chicago Tribune*, 7 October 1997.
13. Carey, interview.

Chapter Twelve

1. Charles P. Carey, interview by Jeffrey L. Rodengen, digital recording, 1 March 2007, Write Stuff Enterprises, Inc.
2. Terry Duffy, interview by Jeffrey L. Rodengen, digital recording, 7 March 2007, Write Stuff Enterprises, Inc.
3. Ibid.
4. Carey, interview.
5. David Greising, "Delivering on a Dream: Merger Secures Chicago's Place as a Worldwide Trading Center," *Chicago Tribune*, 18 October 2006.
6. Duffy, interview.
7. Ibid.
8. Carey, interview.
9. Duffy, interview.
10. Ibid.
11. Carey, interview.
12. Ibid.
13. Duffy, interview.
14. Matt Krantz, "Commodities Traders in Chicago Join Forces," *USA Today*, 18 October 2006.

15. Kopin Tan, "Windfall in the Windy City," *Barron's*, October 23 2006.
16. "Chicago's New Powerhouse," *Chicago Tribune*, 18 October 2006.
17. Aaron Lucchetti, Alistair MacDonald, and Edward Taylor, "Futures Shock: Chicago Merc to Buy Board of Trade," *Wall Street Journal*, 18 October 2006.
18. David Roeder, "Exchanging Vows: CBOT Says 'I Do' to $8 Billion Merger Offer from Merc," *Chicago Sun-Times*, 18 October 2006.
19. Duffy, interview.
20. David Greising, "Delivering on a Dream," *Chicago Tribune*, 18 October 2006.
21. Carey, interview.
22. Duffy, interview.
23. David Roeder, "How Will These Guys Fit the Merc Here?" *Chicago Sun-Times*, 25 October 2006.
24. Duffy, interview.
25. Lucchetti, MacDonald, and Taylor, "Futures Shock."
26. Duffy, interview.
27. Greg Burns and Susan Chandler, "Long Division: Is It Over?" *Chicago Tribune*, 22 October 2006.
28. Carey, interview.
29. Ibid.
30. Ibid.
31. Duffy, interview.
32. James Grant, "Innovate or Die," *Wall Street Journal*, 21 October 2006.
33. CME Press Release, "CME Outlines Why ICE Proposal Is Inferior to CME/CBOT Merger Agreement," 22 March 2007.
34. CME Press Release, "CME and CBOT Receive U.S. Department of Justice Clearance to Proceed with Merger," 11 June 2007.
35. CME Press Release, "CME and CBOT Complete Merger Creating the Leading Global Financial Exchange," 12 July 2007.

INDEX

Page numbers in italics indicate photographs